HIDE & SEEK

DISCOVER THE AWE
OF BEING YOU

KARRI BRUNTZ

ACE OF SPADES PRESS

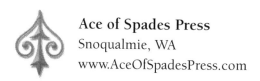

Ace of Spades Press
Snoqualmie, WA
www.AceOfSpadesPress.com

© 2015 Karri Bruntz

ISBN: 978-0-69231-172-1

COVER DESIGN: Tristan Von Elrik • www.imaginaria-studios.com
INTERIOR DESIGN: Gary A. Rosenberg • www.thebookcouple.com
AUTHOR PHOTOS: Leo Lam • www.leolam.com

Printed in the United States of America

CONTENTS

MASTERY GUIDE

1 | Maximize Your Impact

2 | Achieve through Alignment

3 | Savor the Journey

4 | Think with Compassion

5 | Engage with Integrity

6 | Retreat for Sanity

YOU Are the Key

ᴵNTRODUCTION

*A*n *odyssey* is defined as a long and eventful or adventurous journey or experience. The game of Hide & Seek you are about
to learn is all about your personal odyssey to success through self-
discovery. Success means something different for every one of us and
thankfully so. Life would be pretty boring if we all had the same ideas,
the same paths, and the same dreams and goals.

The word *awe* means a feeling of reverence and admiration, mixed
with fear or wonder, produced by that which is grand, sublime, and
extremely powerful. *Hide & Seek* is about helping you discover the awe
of being you! You *are* grand, sublime, and extremely powerful. Yet you
have likely experienced the feelings of fear and wonder at some point.

Why would you fear yourself? It's actually very common. Most of
us don't really know who we are. Most of us spend years, even life-
times, searching for answers that will give us peace of mind and feelings of fulfillment.

I've spent the last two decades of my life passionately seeking—
seeking the processes, the habits, the thought patterns, the products,
the people, and my own personal connection to authenticity to find the
meaning of true success—the feeling of awe—in my life. I've also spent
countless hours studying other successful individuals to see where the
various formulas for success intersect. I've discovered that there is a
pattern woven throughout all the different formulas for success, and
the common characteristic at the root of that pattern is authenticity.

Being authentic is not always as easy as it may seem. Living up to someone else's standards, trying to conform to what society says is appropriate, or allowing self-imposed beliefs to guide our actions— even when it makes us feel horrible—are just a few of the ways we hide our authentic Self. And hiding the part of you that is most natural and real takes a lot of energy. It ultimately leaves you feeling unhappy, unhealthy, unclear, and unfulfilled.

How do I know this? Because I've lived it. I was going through life reactively and trying to find the success, the person, the feeling, the product, the . . . thing that would make me happy. I had everything that looked like success from the outside looking in: a beautiful home, a great husband, lots of money, and loving family and friends, just to name a few. Yet, I vividly remember sitting on my deck with a friend and saying, "I have such an amazing life, but I'm just not happy."

I now know that what was missing was my connection to the real me, my true center. My own genuine authenticity had been hidden from me! Once I discovered the authentic me, I realized it was what I'd been seeking my whole life. Authenticity is the key to fulfillment and success, both personally and professionally.

It took many life-changing moments for the real me to fully surface. One of the most memorable ones took place when my son Taylor was just a little guy. I was a divorced, single mom at the time. I had started my own business as a financial advisor a couple of years earlier and was enjoying success in the typical "business" sense of the word. I was making great money, I was building a solid business, and I thought I was successfully juggling my personal responsibilities of a little one with the professional responsibilities of the business.

Little did I know that the freight train was coming, and I was standing on the tracks with earplugs in. I didn't date much then (there wasn't a whole lot of extra time), yet I was wrapped up in drama from some of my . . . shall we say, not so great, choices. The freight train was building speed, and loaded onto that train were poor health choices, undesirable situations, and the stresses of being a single mom and a sole business owner. Even worse, I was carelessly standing on the tracks with no sense of awareness.

Looking back, it's interesting to note that just before all hell broke loose, I had found the love of my life, and everything from my business to my personal life was finally feeling fantastic. Just a couple of months later, however, the train and I collided. It showed up for me as extreme fatigue. I couldn't work. In fact, I couldn't do much of anything other than sleep and rest. There were days when all I could do was drop my son off at school, stop by the grocery store to pick up something to eat, and then head home to spend the rest of the day in bed.

The doctor began running every test imaginable and found that my liver enzymes were slightly elevated. This led to more tests and the conclusion that it *might* be autoimmune liver disease. I bought a book about the disease (information on the Internet was not as accessible as it is today) and read that the prognosis is approximately ten years to live. It felt like my heart stopped. The idea that I would not get to see my son grow up, go to college, or get married was heartrending. I felt deep despair. I was scared and sad, and I didn't know what to do. I vividly remember the tears and the gut-wrenching pain when I thought about the reality of my life being over by the time I was in my midthirties.

Then it was as if a voice inside me said, "You don't have to accept this reality if you don't want to."

It was in that moment that I felt myself make a choice: A choice to take control and stand in my own power. A choice to connect and seek out whatever it took to understand what was happening to my body and why. A choice that not only changed my life forever, but ignited a flame inside me to help others discover the power of choice as well.

I began seeking anyone and any form of knowledge that would help me discover what was happening to me. I began learning about "alternative" health practices, how to eat a healthier diet, and about the direct connection between mind and body. I was open to anything.

And through it all, I learned to begin trusting my own intuition to know which direction to follow.

Only a couple of weeks after I made this choice, I found a Traditional Chinese Medicine doctor through some friends in Vancouver, Canada, and made the trek from Seattle to see him. He knew nothing of my situation. He pinched the skin on my forearm, checked my pulse (a technique to read meridians, or energy channels, throughout the body), and looked at my tongue. From that two-minute evaluation, he drew the outline of a body on a piece of scratch paper with a blackened circle where the liver would be. In broken English, he said, "Your *Chi* is stuck in your liver."

I was flabbergasted! How did this guy nail my issue with such little information or testing? The answer didn't seem important. Without a second thought, I blurted out what I really wanted to know: "Why?"

His response will remain with me forever. The simplistic complexity of it is the basis for my wholehearted belief that awareness is the key to living an authentic and successful life. He said, "Stress."

Stress! Really? That's it? Stress is the cause of something that has the potential to kill me in ten years? Stress is the reason I may not see my son grow into a man? Stress is the root of my problems? I was ecstatic! I knew that if stress was the problem, then I had the power to change it. I had the power to make choices to reduce stress in my life and change my course. The questions began to flood my mind . . .

What, or who, is causing stress in my life?

How is my body connected to the stress I've been feeling emotionally?

Is my diet related to this stress?

Where can I learn more about how to reduce stress in my life?

Who can help me? Who do I know who might be able to offer a different point of view than the one the mainstream doctors have been offering me?

Introduction

Does my physical body express symptoms that come from an emotional problem or a mental one?

How can I stay open to new ideas and opportunities that increase my awareness and my connection to something deeper than the everyday activities of my life?

Through those questions, I was able to increase not only my awareness of myself but also an awareness that life is a constant process—a game, if you will—where we are seeking fulfillment, happiness, and understanding.

During this same process of opening up and creating a broader awareness about the bigger picture and connections between resistance and disease, I remember thinking that my life had been better than ever before when I collided with the "stress train." What was that all about? Why did this all happen when I finally had my "shitake" together? What I learned over time is that after our bodies have been in "survival mode," when we finally let down our guard, the repercussions of survival mode often show up. Our bodies are amazing in their ability to cope with what we experience in life. But because we are energetic beings and energy must move continuously, the physical, mental, or emotional stress we experience has to be released or it will remain trapped and show up as some form of illness.

My first proof of this energy-moving principle came within a month of my appointment with the wise Chinese doctor when my health turned around. My liver enzymes went back to normal and my energy returned. This was the first sign of my efforts to reduce stress in my life. Along with making a trek up to the Chinese doc every week for acupuncture and cupping (an ancient technique where they put suction cups on your skin that are designed to get your Chi moving), I took some herbal remedies he prescribed to support my liver.

I also started learning how to eat healthily. I remember reading many books, writing down a huge list of foods (some I'd never heard of, like arrowroot), and spending four hours at the local natural grocery store perusing the items down every aisle. I immersed myself in the process of learning how to eat healthier foods and the reasons for doing it. I was determined to figure out how I could support my body toward vitality and health.

Let me just make a quick side note here: I didn't start eating salad without dressing and bland rice cakes. I wanted to continue eating foods that tasted good to me, but were also good for my body. This process actually took many years to fully understand. Through trial and error, I have been able to find a beautiful balance when it comes to food. I still go through phases when I just want sugar! I can eat an entire medium pizza, and I sometimes crave chocolate like my life is depending on it. I've learned that these phases are just part of life, and if I try to fight them, they'll only get bigger. I've also learned that when I accept them and welcome them in as part of my experience, they soon pass and I don't get derailed by them.

The trips to the Chinese doc, the herbal remedies, and the food changes were just part of the equation. There were still years of learning and self-discovery ahead of me and layers upon layers to peel away. This experience was simply the wakeup call I needed to show me how important it was to be fully aware of my thoughts, beliefs, and actions. This growing awareness of who I am at my core and what is most important to me was my first glimpse of awe in seeing my authentic Self.

This awareness is what I want to explore with you! An awareness of who you are and what you want out of your life. You wouldn't have picked up this book if you weren't longing to better yourself and create a life filled with success, whatever that means to you. Success may be financial rewards or it may be feeling a sense of peace within. It looks different for each one of us, but one thing is certain, success in all forms depends upon your level of authenticity. Living a life in alignment with who you are at the core of your being is the basic formula for success. Awareness leads you to that alignment. Together, they create authenticity, the key to a fulfilled life.

As we explore a new take on the game of Hide & Seek together, my deepest desire is that you will find your authentic Self and step into your own power to create a life of joy, fulfillment, fun, and success. I've been on this awareness path for many years, and there's one thing I know for sure: To find the success and personal fulfillment you desire, you have to take an active role in the process.

CREATE YOUR PERSONAL RULEBOOK

As you read through *Hide & Seek*, you will see **Personal Rulebook Play** sections. These activities allow you to think about the concept presented and apply it to your personal situation. *Hide & Seek* is designed to be interactive. Just reading through the material can leave you thinking, *That's a really cool concept, and there were some great ideas in there.* The problem with that approach is that, if you are like 98 percent of the population, you will then put the book down, go back to the busyness of your life, and forget most of it.

We learn through experience. We learn by doing. We learn by connecting a concept to something that is tangible in our own lives. So if you really want to get the most out of the concepts and ideas you learn in this book, **please do the Personal Rulebook Plays!** As you will learn in the pages to follow, when you are inspired, it is the time to act. Inspired action leads to fulfillment and success. You are reading this book because you are ready to be inspired and to create a life that is rooted in authenticity.

As we move through your games of Hide & Seek (yes, there will be *many* games), I will be with you, guiding you by asking questions to prompt and focus your awareness, and by the time we finish, you will be able to continue developing your Personal Rulebook on your own as you experience life with a new perspective. So let's start right now. Get out a notebook, your iPad, laptop, or phone and begin creating your own rulebook. Three simple steps will help get you started:

Step 1 PERSONALIZE YOUR RULEBOOK

Put your name at the top of the first page (or on the cover) like this:

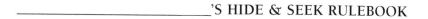

_____'S HIDE & SEEK RULEBOOK

In my case, it would say, KARRI'S HIDE & SEEK RULEBOOK. You're titling it with your name because this game is all about you. It doesn't have anything to do with your family, your friends, your colleagues, or anyone else for that matter. I'm not saying your game doesn't involve them, but I am saying your Rulebook is specific to you. For example, there are going to be rules for you that will be different from the rules in your partner's rulebook.

Different rules for each of us in the Hide & Seek games are essential because each of us brings unique strengths and perspectives to the game. If you are trying to play your game by your partner's rules, it's like trying to play a game of volleyball by a basketball rulebook. It's no wonder you may end up feeling unsuccessful, confused, and sometimes hurt.

Step 2 STATE YOUR PURPOSE

After you've personalized your rulebook, write the following statement in bold letters:

> **PURPOSE: The purpose of my Hide & Seek games is to discover the awe of being Me. Who I am, what I do best, what I need, what strengths I bring, what I enjoy, who I enjoy being with, what I want to spend my time doing, and how I want to feel. As I learn how to use these preferences, I will align myself—and my actions—with them so I can create a life of personal and professional success.**

This statement is simply your starting point. You are free to change it however you want with the understanding that the purpose of *Hide & Seek* is to find your authentic Self, always. Every game has an outcome, and this game's only outcome is seeking the *You* within and bringing that authentic *You* into every area, every situation, and every moment of your life.

Step 3   CREATE YOUR PERSONAL RULEBOOK PLAYS

As you read, you'll be creating Personal Rulebook Plays that you will identify along the way. Each time you get to a new Play, label it at the top of a new page in your Personal Rulebook like this: *Personal Rulebook Play: Title of Play.* Do this each time you encounter a new Rulebook Play so that you can keep track of your progress throughout the book.

That's it! You are on your way to learning a new game that has the potential to bring you deep contentment and great joy, along with every form of success you desire. You are about to see how much fun your life can be when you make your life your playground. Thank you for allowing me to be a part of your odyssey. May you enjoy the adventure and be grateful for the eventfulness of the journey, and through the fear and wonder, you will discover the awe of being you.

Kari

CHAPTER ONE

THE GAME

*R*emember when you were a kid—when life was about playing with friends, going to the swimming pool, and using your imagination to create whatever your heart desired? When life was all about being in the present moment? When days, weeks, and months did not fly by because your calendar was packed with commitments, but instead the summers felt long? Life was simple. It was about doing what you wanted to do and being who you wanted to be each and every day.

While I understand that every child didn't grow up in the Beaver Cleaver family, I also believe that each one of us is born with a magical essence that is at the very core of our being. This essence is the very nature of who we are. It is the force within us that keeps us alive, engaged, and curious.

> *Each one of us is born with a magical essence*
> *that is at the very core of our being.*

I was born and raised in a small town in Nebraska. We didn't have to lock our doors at night. We slept with the windows open and could leave our keys in the car when we ran into the store for groceries. It was a wonderful place to grow up. Summers were long. Most days involved riding my bike across town to spend the afternoon at the public swimming pool, jumping off the high diving board, finding friends in the pool for Marco Polo, and dreaming during the rest periods of being a lifeguard one day when I was older.

The evenings though, *ahh* . . . that is when the neighborhood came alive! We would round up all of our friends, boys and girls, old and young, and pick teams for an exciting game of Hide & Seek. Those memories contain excitement, challenge, and a little pain. I still have a dent in my right shin from running one night into the new deck my dad build in our backyard. Holy bejesus, that hurt.

We would set the entire block as the boundaries, choose the home base, and join "forces" to win the game. As the seeking team began to count "one one-thousand, two one-thousand, three one-thousand," the hiding team would scatter to find places to hide, the feelings of anticipation building inside them while they waited to be found.

We spent hours searching for new hiding places, chasing each other, and sneaking up to home base to try to rescue our teammates who had been caught. We lived for the thrill of the chase, the satisfaction of the catch, the disappointment of being caught, and the exhilaration of freeing and being freed. All of these emotions and experiences from a game—a simple game that allowed each of us the opportunity to have fun, to be challenged, to use our physical and mental abilities, and to connect to our essence.

Children love games because games allow us to tap into the essence of who we are. Through games, we're able to release any limiting thoughts that create resistance in our lives. They let us use our five senses to connect with an experience and find joy in being present, and even give us the chance to discover the keen intuitive power of our perceptive sixth sense.

Adults love games, too. Why? Because games allow us to connect with our inner child. They take us back to those raw emotions we were willing to experience as a kid. They bring us into the present moment. They challenge us to use our physical, mental, emotional, and even spiritual muscles. They fuel our competitive desires and drive us to expand as individuals. They captivate us with excitement, suspense, and disappointment.

Games allow us to connect with our inner child.
They take us back to those raw emotions
we were willing to experience as a kid.

Think about a football stadium filled with tens of thousands of people all acting like children—screaming, yelling, and giving high-fives. Some with funny hats, some with no shirts and body paint, and almost all decked out in their team's colors. Where else do you find this many *adults* who are willing to act so differently from the way they act in the rest of their lives? This behavior we'd call "crazy" anywhere else is mutually acceptable to everyone in the stadium! Can you imagine someone dressing or acting at work the same way they do at a football game? They would be fired or at least gossiped about.

Why do they do it? Why do people love the experience of games? Why do they allow themselves and others to behave in ways that would normally be considered "socially unacceptable"?

Because it's fun! Because at the core of our nature, we each want to enjoy life. Because the best parts of life are being able to feel unrestricted, to know we can be who we are while feeling the freedom of acceptance, and to feel the confidence that comes from successfully overcoming a challenge.

Even though in some games the athletes may be the people who are acting out the challenge at hand, games show us that we are all intimately—and energetically—connected to one another. This is easily seen during a game with fans cheering on athletes. The fans are an integral part of the game and oftentimes help shift the momentum.

Understanding this phenomenon of momentum in such a tangible way can teach us how to use it in daily life. This is just one way that games teach you about the personal playground you are in every day . . . the playground of your life.

COME OUT, COME OUT, WHEREVER YOU ARE

You play a game every day. It's called the game of life. It is a game that is very similar to that cherished childhood game of Hide & Seek. There is also a master key within this particular game of Hide & Seek, which you will learn as you go through these pages. This key reveals the way in which you always win the game. The key is what unlocks the door to your personal and professional success. It opens the door, shedding light on what seems a mystery to most. Those who are most successful in life have discovered it and use it every day.

The difference between the childhood game of Hide & Seek and this game of Hide & Seek is that you are not only "seeking" but *You* are also the one "hiding." I know, you may be thinking, *Hold it one second! What do you mean, I'm the one hiding?* In this game, the hiding *You* I am referring to is the *You* at your core, your true Self, your Soul, the force within you that is your essence.

Have you ever wondered, "Why am I here? What is the purpose of my life? What will make me happy?" Millions of people today and throughout history have asked these questions, not because they are easy, but because they are at the very heart of our existence.

Your entire life is a game of Hide & Seek with yourself. It is the ultimate and continuous calling of "Come out, come out, wherever you are!" It's the experience of finding out who you are, discovering who you want to be, and believing in your value and worth. It is discovering your authentic Self and experiencing the contentment that comes from settling into that place of peace within you. Whether you would consider yourself spiritual or not, it is undeniable that there is an innate force within you that is the very nature of who you are.

Without it, your brain stops thinking, your heart stops beating, your lungs stop breathing, and the energy that is you moves from your body into the nonphysical world. In fact, when someone takes his or her last breath, those who have shared this profound experience say there is no doubt their loved one is no longer in his or her physical body, yet oftentimes they report still feeling their loved one's presence around them.

Who—or what—is this presence that is the authentic *You*? Well, that's where the fun of your games of Hide & Seek comes in. You will discover it in the situations you love most and also in those that challenge you. You'll discover it through the people around you who make you feel good and also through the ones who rub you the wrong way. It will reveal itself through your awareness of places where you feel relaxed and comfortable, as well as those where you feel unsettled. You will find it in activities that are exciting to you and in others that leave you frustrated or fearful. These are all aspects of *seeking* the real *You*.

Each of these situations, or life experiences, gives you the chance to go seeking, to play in a new game with different surroundings and different players, but always seeking the same *You*. You are about to make your life your playground. By changing your perspective to one of playfulness and fun, you will allow for the real you to come out and play. When you can be more lighthearted about your life, you will discover the wonder in being you, rather than feeling fearful about what you may find.

CHAPTER TWO

THE RULES

*T*he real fun of the game comes when you learn to develop a level of mastery in the different areas of your Hide & Seek games. As you've learned, it's a process of calling, "Come out, come out, wherever you are!" to your authentic Self and living your life in alignment. Just as you searched for your friends as a kid, you now get to search for yourself as an adult. It's a game that gets played over and over again in all kinds of situations.

One game might be at work with your team, when you are trying to find your place and have a voice in a challenging project. Another might be with family, where everyone's different opinions are giving you an opportunity to stand in your own power. And yet another game might even be with friends, when you are trying to navigate the social dynamics of a group and wondering how the heck you fit in.

The situations are endless, and the opportunities for you to develop a level of mastery are abundant. Personal values and beliefs, interpersonal relationships and interactions, and even business situations all present new games of Hide & Seek for becoming a master of your personal and professional life.

Master is defined as a skilled practitioner of a particular art or activity. We are going to explore how you can become a master of the art called your life. To do so, there are six aspects we will cover that lead to the authentic *You*. And as you will see, when you live your life connected with the essence of who you are, you will feel the contentment and joy that automatically flows into your experience.

The following six aspects make up a MASTER:

⤺ **M**aximize Your Impact

⤺ **A**chieve through Alignment

⤺ **S**avor the Journey

⤺ **T**hink with Compassion

⤺ **E**ngage with Integrity

⤺ **R**etreat for Sanity

As we go through each part of *Hide & Seek,* you will learn some specific tools and processes within each chapter and develop skills to help you apply them in your life. Understanding is only the first part of the equation. Developing a level of mastery happens when you know how to implement that understanding into your experience. We learn through experience, not just intellectual understanding.

When you combine the six aspects listed above (M-A-S-T-E-R) with *You*, it creates MASTERY. Finding *You* is crucial to personal mastery. *You* are the key to MASTERY. When you intimately know your authentic Self, and you know how to live in alignment with that Self, you will achieve a level of mastery in your life.

By practicing the ideas and processes described, you will discover how to skillfully balance the MASTERY characteristics and achieve true fulfillment in life—at work, at home, in relationships, and within yourself.

⤺ **M**aximize Your Impact

⤺ **A**chieve through Alignment

⤺ **S**avor the Journey

⤺ **T**hink with Compassion

⤺ **E**ngage with Integrity

⤺ **R**etreat for Sanity

⤺ *YOU* **Are the Key**

Becoming a master of your life and developing a level of mastery is the gist of the Hide & Seek game you are playing with *You*. Becoming a skilled practitioner of the art of *You* brings you what most people are seeking in their lives: happiness, a sense of purpose, success, health, contentment, awareness, self-respect, self-worth, and confidence.

Unfortunately, many people end up feeling lost, disappointed, unhappy, and alone because they don't even realize they're playing a game. They go through life reacting to whatever flows in and out of their day with no definite sense of purpose or desire. They don't even realize that life is setting them up for outstanding success, if they could just understand the game, know their role in it, and take a bird's-eye view. They spend time focused on whatever is in their immediate view rather than looking at the whole picture to find opportunities to win. It's like a quarterback who's focused on the 250-pound linebacker coming at him instead of his three teammates who are open for easy touchdowns.

As with any game, you must know the rules before you can master it, or you may end up feeling flattened by that 250-pound linebacker. The rules of your lifelong MASTERY game of Hide & Seek are very similar to your childhood game of Hide & Seek:

1. Determine who is "IT."
2. Designate the boundaries.
3. Decide on the location of home base.
4. Acknowledge "Olly Olly Oxen Free."
5. Start counting and . . . "GAME ON!"

Rule #1
DETERMINE WHO IS "IT"

The first rule of the game is determining who is IT. In your MASTERY game of Hide & Seek, you are *always* IT. Life is about your individual journey. The purpose of your life is to discover everything you can about yourself: to find out who you are and who you are not, what you do best and what you're lousy at, what you desire or detest, and what you want or don't want. It is a natural process of exploring the balance of polar opposites in your world. And there are endless opportunities to find your own personal preferences.

"You're IT!"

You're IT because you are the one seeking the real *You* that is hidden behind perceptions and beliefs. You get to search for the real *You* in every situation and seek out your authentic Self. While the searching must be a personal quest to find truly meaningful answers, you don't have to do it alone. Thankfully, this MASTERY game of Hide & Seek is a team sport. You are the captain, and you get to choose the players you want on your team to help you seek.

How empowering to know you are in charge! You get to choose who will help you during each game you play. Your team may include family members, friends, a coach, a therapist, or a random stranger on an airplane with whom you have an enlightening conversation. The world is full of potential teammates who are all available to assist you in the hunt. They will be there to provide feedback, to walk with you, and to reflect insights along the way. As the captain though, you are the one who gets to make the final call and determine what choice is best for you.

The Outcomes of Being IT: Self-Awareness and Self-Confidence

The two outcomes of being IT—and playing the game—are self-awareness and self-confidence. These two results alone have the power to change your life into an extraordinary experience. Awareness is composed of understanding and learning. It is a never-ending curiosity. When you remain curious, you stay open to possibilities.

Experiencing these possibilities teaches you how to master your life.

Self-confidence comes from confiding in yourself; this is empowerment. It is realigning moment to moment with what you know in your gut to be right. Confidence comes when you honor your own point of view, when you celebrate your authentic Self in any given moment. It is through this realization that you will develop a deep-seated self-confidence that will guide you on your quest for personal mastery.

Confidence comes when you honor your own point of view, when you celebrate your authentic Self in any given moment.

Being IT requires being open to awareness and confidence if you want to win the game. Don't worry or condemn yourself if you miss an opportunity though. There will always be another game to practice becoming a master. Remember, the purpose of life is about your journey. Every game is just another part of your journey to seek, to learn, and to grow.

Identifying Your Needs and Strengths

Your MASTERY games of Hide & Seek are designed to help you get to know yourself better than ever before, and part of being "IT" is becoming intimately familiar with you. As you become more aware of who you are, you must get up close and personal with two things: The first is your needs. The second is your strengths. Two systems that are, in my opinion, fantastic approaches for defining our personal needs and strengths are Human Needs Psychology (developed by Tony Robbins and Cloe Madanes) and StrengthsFinder (developed by Don Clifton and adopted by the Gallup organization). These systems give you a framework to better understand who you are and give you a point of focus as you play your MASTERY games.

Know Your Needs

According to the Robbins-Madanes Training Center, Human Needs Psychology is based on the premise that we all have "six human needs, or fundamental drives within each of us, that compel us forward in a quest to experience a life of meaning." We automatically act to satisfy these primal needs without even consciously trying. This means that your actions and desires are motivated by deep underlying needs. Ever wonder *why* you do what you do? This insight into what motivates you can have a huge impact on your actions or lack thereof. Human Needs Psychology explains that motivation is always traced back to a need you are trying to fulfill. We may all choose different ways to fulfill these needs, but every action we take can be traced back to one or more of the following needs: Certainty, Uncertainty/Variety, Significance, Love, Growth, and Contribution.

We all have each of the six needs at some level, but their order of importance is unique to each of us. The following definitions will give you a glimpse into each need so that you can think about how they stack up in your life.

1. **Certainty:** The need for security, stability, and reliability.

2. **Uncertainty/Variety:** The need for change, stimulation, and challenge.

3. **Significance:** The need to feel acknowledged, recognized, and valued.

4. **Love and Connection:** The need to love, to feel loved, and to feel connection with others.

5. **Growth:** The need to grow, improve, and develop, both in character and in spirit.

6. **Contribution:** The need to give, to help others, and to make a difference.

When you are able to see how these needs influence the choices you make and the actions you take, you begin to see yourself—and others—in a whole new light. For instance, if Significance is one of your primary needs, you will understand why you might be driven to be number one at everything you do. Or, if Contribution is at the top of your list, you recognize that your relentless desire to help others is just part of your makeup. When you can see that a basic driving need, like Uncertainty, can create a person who loves to explore the world and lives for variety in his life, you may be able to appreciate who he is and his adventurous nature. The same appreciation is true when you are dealing with someone who desperately needs Certainty in her life, and she struggles with branching out or trying something new.

What I love most about the Human Needs Psychology approach is that it gives us a choice to come from the perspective of curiosity and acceptance of ourselves and those around us. When we understand that we are making choices because they are meeting our primary needs, it helps us appreciate and try to understand our actions or choices rather than judge them. Through understanding, you are able to become more aware of the reasons why you do the things you do and why you are the way you are.

It is also important to note that your needs can be serving you, or they can be detrimental to your personal well-being. Have you ever asked yourself, "Why do I keep doing this?" Now that you know the six human needs approach, ask yourself that question again and see which need you are meeting through the habitual actions you are taking. That need is likely in your top two.

Personal Rulebook Play
MY TOP TWO NEEDS

Let's take a closer look during the first Personal Rulebook Play at your top two needs. I'm going to give you a couple of examples during this Play to help you get started. Get out your Personal Rulebook and write down: **Personal Rulebook Play—My Top Two Needs.**

Look at the definitions of each need listed above and spend a little time thinking about which needs are most influential in motivating your actions. For instance, is it Significance? Certainty? Growth?

✦ Which two needs do you believe motivate the majority of your actions? (What are your top two?)

✦ Write down how these top two needs show up in your life. Describe how your actions or choices are fulfilling each need. For instance, "Certainty shows up in my life because I always want to have a plan, and it bothers me when things don't go as I intended."

NEED #1

How it shows up:

How it shows up:

NEED #2

How it shows up:

How it shows up:

✦ What are three ways your top two needs serve you in a positive way? For example, "My need for Significance drives me to achieve in my life, which brings me a wonderful income."

✦ What are three ways these needs do *not* serve you in creating a successful life? For example, "My need for Significance creates a longing to feel worthy of what I consider 'success,' and often leaves me feeling like I have to prove I deserve my prosperity."

Congratulations! You have just completed your first Personal Rulebook Play. You now have a better understanding about who you are and why you do the things you do. You can take this newfound awareness and use it within your Hide & Seek games and in your life. Each time, simply ask yourself, "What need am I trying to fulfill here?" You are playing a game of Hide & Seek to discover more about yourself and to find satisfaction in your life.

Remember, your life is a game and you can have fun with it. If you find that your top two needs are more harmful to your personal happiness, you aren't stuck with them. You can choose to change the order of your six needs whenever you want. Having this new insight can give you the freedom to begin creating the life you want by making new choices rather than living on autopilot and continuing to get the same disappointing results.

A little side note here: Cloe Madanes developed a test to help people uncover their personal order of importance of the six human needs. If you would like to dive into the six human needs in more depth you can find it at www.robbinsmadanescoachtraining.com/six-human-needs-test. Tony Robbins also teaches these needs and demonstrates his mastery of understanding how they show up, and he motivates individuals at his events through "interventions" with participants. It is quite fascinating to watch!

Know Your Strengths

While your needs give you one level of insight about who you are and why you do what you do, your strengths give you similar insight from another perspective. StrengthsFinder is a system based on the idea that we are each born with characteristics, or strengths, that energize us. The best word I know to describe how to determine whether or not you are playing to your strengths is *energized*. When you act from your strengths, you are excited to get started, you finish feeling better than when you started, and you can't wait to come back to the activity.

We are each born with innate gifts. For example, some people are gifted in music, some have a natural tendency to look at a situation and find solutions, and others are able to connect through remarkable relationships skills. There is not one person on the face of the planet who doesn't have strengths, and these strengths are with us from the day we are born until the day we die.

The strengths concept was initially created by Dr. Don Clifton, a professor of educational psychology at the University of Nebraska–Lincoln, who is known as "the Father of Strengths Psychology." Clifton believed that if people would stop focusing on their weaknesses and begin to focus on their innate strengths, they would be able to achieve greater success in life. The Gallup Organization now continues Dr. Clifton's work through the StrengthsFinder assessment. This assessment, which has led millions of people around the world to discover their strengths, reveals thirty-four themes or strengths. These themes include characteristics like strategic, maximizer, connection, communication, learner, responsibility, and empathy, just to name a few.

One of the most telling results related to strengths from studies that have been conducted in corporate America is that 98 percent of people in the workforce are not playing to their strengths most of their day. Ninety-eight percent! That means only 2 percent of people in the working population are actually doing activities during the majority of their day that strengthen them. Can you imagine what this means for productivity? Do you think people are at their best when they are doing something that drains them? Can you see that doing activities during your work hours that feel good to you would make you more successful—not only in your job but from a personal fulfillment perspective as well? Do you think companies would increase their bottom lines and have much happier employees if these companies were enabling their employees to use all of the innate gifts that they bring to the table?

Now that I've got you thinking, let's take a look at how knowing your strengths applies to your MASTERY games of Hide & Seek. Your strengths are the physical representations of who you are. Your strengths help you get to know yourself better, and even more important, they help you appreciate yourself more.

A master is someone who has great knowledge and understanding. You become a master of your life by understanding you. Knowing your innate strengths, appreciating them, and learning how to use them are part of your odyssey. Whether you choose to pay the fee for the Gallup StrengthsFinder test to learn your top five strengths or not, you can learn more about your own strengths by knowing the following truths:

When you are playing to your strengths:

- You lose track of time.

- You feel energized.

- You don't want to stop doing the activity.

- You can't wait to get back to the activity.

- It strengthens you and you feel empowered.

Notice the last statement in this list: *It strengthens you*. There are many things in life that you may be good at, but if those are things that deplete you, then they are *not* your innate and natural strengths. This was a huge revelation for me personally. I tend to have an attitude that I can do anything I put my mind to. This belief has allowed me to achieve great things in my life as well as take on challenges that may seem out of place. I remember learning how to work with html, Photoshop, and "nerdy" software so I could design and manage my own website.

The problem with this "can do" attitude is that I ended up spending hours—we're talking staying up until 3:00 a.m. kind of hours—working on website design. This was a problem because I was completely disconnected from my family, which didn't bode well for my relationship with my hubby and kids. I was spending countless hours hunched over a computer, which led to neck and back problems. And I was stressed out and tired all the time. I was good at what I was doing, but it was completely draining me and leaving a path of destruction when all was said and done.

Personal Rulebook Play
MY STRENGTHS

Just as you did in your first Personal Rulebook Play, write down the following: **Personal Rulebook Play: My Strengths**. Now consider and answer the following questions to help familiarize yourself with your strengths.

Depleting Activities

✦ Can you think about activities in your life that you may be good at, but leave you feeling drained?

✦ What are these activities?

✦ What is it about these activities that drains you?

✦ What is the "cost" to you for keeping these activities in your life? Your relationships? Your energy? Your happiness?

✦ How could you adjust your approach to delegate, or eliminate, these activities from your life?

Strengthening Activities

✦ Can you think about activities that strengthen you, that you are good at, and that leave you feeling energized?

✦ What do you enjoy most about these activities?

✦ How do you feel they strengthen you when you do them?

✦ What are the benefits you experience?

✦ What are the benefits others experience when you are playing to your strengths?

✦ How can you spend more of your time playing to your strengths in your life? At work? At home?

A quick note: I am not trying to say that you should never do depleting activities. Some of these may be very important to the sustainability of your life. Just try to make it a goal to limit the activities that weaken you and increase those that energize you.

If you'd like to learn more about the strengths approach, you can go to www.gallupstrengthscenter.com and purchase the Strengths-Finder test. After taking the online test, you will receive a description of each of your top five strengths. Going further into understanding these strengths and how to use them is another book altogether. In fact, I've spent full-day trainings with companies just teaching individuals how to understand strengths and effectively use them. To begin with a basic understanding though, you can simply go to the Gallup Strengths Center site and explore. Think of it as one of your MASTERY games of Hide & Seek to create greater self-awareness leading you to successfully seek the *You* that is hiding. You can also visit my blog, www.karribruntz.com, to find articles and links to more information about how to discover your strengths.

Rule # 2
DESIGNATE THE BOUNDARIES

Now that you know "You're IT," it is time to figure out the boundaries of your game. Boundaries in the childhood game of Hide & Seek refer to the physical boundaries in which the teams will play during the course of the game. For your MASTERY games of Hide & Seek, the boundaries have a broader meaning. These boundaries reside in the mental, physical, emotional, and spiritual fields. Combining these four areas creates profound boundaries that allow you to become a master. The challenge is knowing where the boundaries are and how—or when—to adjust them.

To put it simply, the boundaries for the MASTERY game of Hide & Seek are:

- ⬳ Focus
- ⬳ Movement
- ⬳ Self-Acceptance
- ⬳ Self-Worth

Understanding how each of these principles guides your game is important to the results you get and, ultimately, your success. These boundaries help create structure for your process to finding the true *You*. Just like a building needs to have a solid foundation, these principles provide the structure to support you on your journey.

The Principle of Focus

Boundaries bring us focus. They show us where we should put our attention. This is the baseline of any game. Without knowing where to focus, you could end up searching the entire town rather than the street block. That means your attention can be spread so thin you have little to no chance of winning the game. It may also mean you are looking in one room of the house when everyone is hiding outside! If your attention is focused away from your desired outcome, there is no chance you are going to reach your goal.

Your ability to focus is your greatest asset. You may not be able to control what is happening to you, who is involved, or even the outcome of a situation, but you can control where you put your focus. This is the most powerful skill we have each been given in our lifelong MASTERY game of Hide & Seek.

---

*You may not be able to control what is happening to you,
who is involved, or even the outcome of a situation,
but you can control where you put your focus.*

Once you realize this skill is completely in your control and you begin to choose where you put your attention, you will see amazing results. Things you desire, goals you want to achieve, and feelings you long to have will all begin to unfold in your life.

Personal Rulebook Play
WHAT I WANT

You don't have to just take my word for the power of focus. Do your own experimenting with this idea. Get out your Personal Rulebook and write down something you want in your life. Start with something simple like, "I want to have a really fun day with my family." Or "I want to enjoy my day at work and feel satisfied with what I accomplish." By directing your focus and being clear on your overall outcome, like having fun with your family or feeling good about your workday, your brain will naturally look for actions throughout the day to satisfy your focus.

Our brains are designed to follow our orders and are wired to find answers. If you tell your brain you want it to find ways to have fun with the family, it will look for ways to have fun with your family. It is continuously looking for opportunities to fulfill your requests throughout your day, and it will continue to find evidence to support the outcome you want. Your brain is always guided by the boundaries of your focus, whether you choose to focus on positive or negative outcomes. You will find that as you explore the power of your focus, you will see for yourself why it is your most powerful skill to manifest things you want in your life.

You will learn more about the process of directing focus and creating tangible results in Chapter 5: Achieve through Alignment, but for now, let's continue on with the next part of designating your boundaries. Boundaries are not just borders. Designating boundaries also refers to instructions about your movement within the game. The principle of movement is crucial to any game, as well as every aspect of your life.

The Principle of Movement

The principle of movement represents change in our life. Change is a constant and never-ending part of our experience. For some, it is embraced. For others, it is feared. One thing is for sure, change is guaranteed, and learning how to handle change is a vital practice of MASTERY.

In your MASTERY games of Hide & Seek, think of change as a multidimensional aspect of your life. It touches every area: physical, mental, emotional, and spiritual. Remember, the goal of the game is to find *You*. Therefore, as you are seeking in any given situation, or game, you want to use the principle of movement to guide your steps. There may be times when it is necessary to remain quiet and alert, while there are other moments when it's time to run! This rule of the game is integral to your success. Knowing when to be still and when to move is the difference between being caught by the seeker and getting away.

For example, let's say that sales are an integral part of your business. I don't know of many businesses that don't rely on sales to succeed, so, if you are active in the professional world, this example will most likely relate to you. The sales process is a delicate dance between the seller and the buyer of a product or service. As you engage with your customer or client, you—the seller—must know when to move and when to step back. There is an exchange of energy, a *change,* that happens during the sales process. If you come on too strong, the buyer will back away. If you don't show how the product or service will benefit the buyer, the exchange of energy (aka the sale) is simply not going to happen.

Those who are best at sales understand this dynamic *and* use their keen senses to navigate the flow of the energy exchange. If the buyer is ready to buy, the successful salesperson knows "the iron is hot" and asks for the order. If the buyer still needs something more, the effective salesperson waits and continues to answer the buyer's questions. By discovering more about the buyer's wants and needs, you are able to "heat up the iron" and strike with a high probability of success.

This is just one example of how you can use the principle of movement in your life. It can be applied to your interactions with your kids, to achieving your personal health goals, or in creating a deeper level of intimacy with your partner.

Have fun applying the principle of movement to the endless Hide & Seek games you'll play throughout your life. The joy is seeking *You* in each of those situations. The game is understanding what will bring you fulfillment, and then bringing that authentic desire into a situation to produce success for you and everyone else involved. When you played Hide & Seek as a child, it was an activity that was fun for you and your friends. Your interactions were crucial to the success of the game. And a successful game simply meant you all had a good time.

Personal Rulebook Play
APPLYING THE PRINCIPLE OF MOVEMENT

Get out your Personal Rulebook. In this play, you will be learning how to apply the principle of movement to your life. Read the questions below and jot down your answers in your rulebook.

+ If change is guaranteed, and your ability to successfully navigate change in your life is simply the ability to know when to be still and when to act, how could you apply this principle?

+ Is there a current situation you feel uncertain about?

+ How would being still, quiet, and alert help you find clarity?

✦ What information do you need to feel ready to embrace this change?

✦ How does the idea of something new feel?

✦ Why do you think you have feelings of doubt or fear (or any other feeling you uncovered)?

Create a plan for moving forward in this situation. Determine if, and when, it will be time to take action. Remember, sometimes choosing *not* to act may actually be the best action. If I could give you one piece of advice on this one, it would be to trust your gut. If something doesn't feel right, there is a reason. Once you've gone through the process of answering the above questions, if moving forward still doesn't feel right, then know that you are not yet ready for this change for one reason or another. Your gut doesn't lie . . . trust it!

The Principle of Self-Acceptance

One of the keys to designating boundaries is being able to recognize when there are imaginary boundaries that are holding you back and releasing those limiting beliefs. How often have you introduced resistance into your experience by saying something like:

"I don't have enough energy to do everything I want to do."

"Girls like that just don't go for guys like me."

"All the good men are already taken."

"I am just not meant to be thin."

"I don't have the education."

"I wasn't raised to believe I can become whatever I want to be."

"I would love to have more money, but I just can't seem to get a break!"

Each of these statements, and others like them, will hold you back from attaining your desires. What you focus on becomes your reality. When you put your attention on a belief that limits you from moving in the direction of success, the limiting belief becomes your experience.

In the childhood game of Hide & Seek, if you focus on the fact that you are not finding anyone, you will walk around the block and pass the other kids who are hiding almost every time. Why? Because you are focused on *not finding* the kids. On the other hand, when you put your focus on what you want to believe (that you are going to find the kids who are hiding), you listen intensely for any sounds, you look around with keen awareness for unusual movement or shapes, and you put all of your attention on what you want to discover. The result, almost every time, is that you zero in on exactly what—or who—you are looking for.

Learning to release limiting beliefs will help you master your personal game of Hide & Seek. When you accept who you are and where you are in your life right now, you give yourself the space to become all that you can be. This isn't meant to sound like a U.S. Army commercial, but it is true. Self-acceptance is the start of a journey of self-discovery that leads to success.

Does that belief ring true for you? I have been learning to accept all that I am for many years now. For the most part, I have done a pretty good job. One of my most recent "aha" moments was discovering one of my huge limiting beliefs. In fact, it was number one on the list above. "I don't have enough energy to do everything I want to do."

I've got big dreams and lots of ideas that drop into my head and inspire me! I not only want to explore these thoughts in my own life, but I also want to share the insights I've discovered to help others find true happiness and fulfillment in their lives. I want to have fabulous relationships with my family and friends. I want to be a kick-ass businesswoman and challenge myself in ways that help me grow. I want to be strong and healthy in my body and mind.

Until recently, I didn't understand that what was holding me back was simply a limiting belief that I don't have enough energy. I was achieving great success by most any standard, but "most any standard" is not *my* standard. By realizing that not having enough energy was just a belief, I was able to step back and seek out the answers that would allow me to have the kind of energy I so desperately wanted.

Personal Rulebook Play
RELEASING MY LIMITING BELIEFS

By releasing limiting beliefs, you remove an invisible shield that keeps you from seeing what you long to find. Think about a limiting belief that might be holding you back and write it down in your Personal Rulebook. Then answer the following questions:

+ What are you missing out on in your life due to this belief?

+ What if this belief was not true?

+ What would your life be like then?

+ How would your life be better if you felt differently?

Be thoughtful with your responses, but don't overthink them. If you are unsure about how to release the hold that this belief has on your life, you can come back to it with the ability to break through it after you have learned how to effectively use Universal Laws later in Chapter 5: Achieve through Alignment. On the other hand, if you are in a place right now where you are able to see that you have a limiting belief that is holding you back from accepting yourself and enjoying your life at the highest possible level and you're ready to just "let it go," feel free to do so. Change, or creating new boundaries, doesn't *have* to be a laborious process. It can be as simple as saying, "I'm ready to start choosing a new belief."

The Principle of Self-Worth

The final principle within the rules of designating boundaries is setting boundaries. This includes boundaries with yourself as well as others. In our childhood game of Hide & Seek we chose our teammates, and just that process of picking teams provided life lessons. If you were the first one chosen versus the last one, there was a different emotional feeling, which may have often been attached to your perception of self-worth. This perception of self-worth may have hinged not only on your order in the pick but also on your game skills. If you were a fast runner, you knew that your contribution to the team would be appreciated and that you would be respected by your teammates, as well as those on the other team. But if you were a slow runner, and perhaps were the last one chosen, you most likely had that disappointed feeling in your gut and developed a belief that you weren't "good enough."

This process of developing respect for yourself is also true in your lifelong MASTERY game of Hide & Seek. In fact, finding the real *You* is all about having respect for yourself and knowing your inherent worthiness. Becoming a master is rooted in accepting nothing less than honor from yourself and from others. If you understood just how precious the being that is *You* is, you would never question it again. Part of your MASTERY game of Hide & Seek is to find the authentic *You* that is so precious. The best word to describe it is awe.

Authentic self-valuing comes naturally to some, but to many it is one of the most difficult concepts to wholeheartedly master. It's okay if you happen to be one who needs some extra coaching on this issue. You are not alone. In fact, you are in company with the majority of people in the world. There is a reason billions of dollars are spent on products, processes, and information designed to help people discover their inherent worth. In general, societies have disconnected from the inherent wholeness that comes from being connected to the Soul within and instead put much of their attention on external factors to reflect their personal value or worth.

But genuine worthiness has nothing to do with money and every-thing to do with the gift of life that lives within each one of us. A high level of self-respect and self-worth shows up as confidence. This is not the kind of ego-centered confidence that is often described as "cocky." Instead, genuine confidence comes from deep within and is rooted in self-love—a self-love that is not "mushy" or soft, but characterized by strength and connection to your fullest potential.

> *Genuine confidence comes from deep within and is rooted in self-love—a self-love that is not "mushy" or soft, but characterized by strength and connection to your fullest potential.*

To win your MASTERY games of Hide & Seek throughout your life, you must set the boundaries of respect. This is a nonnegotiable expectation that becomes a standard for those you interact with and, even more important, your internal dialogue. Your internal dialogue, or self-talk, is one of the key factors in your success. The quote "what you believe you will achieve" is famous because it is true!

Self-worth leads to self-respect. Self-respect leads to self-confidence. Self-confidence leads to success. So if you want to achieve success in your life, you start by accepting who you are and believing that you deserve anything you desire. This may sound like a really big feat to you. In fact, the majority of us struggle, at some level, to believe we are worthy of success, love, and acceptance. Let me assure you, the promise of finding that worth lies in your ability to become a master and win when you play Hide & Seek. It is when you find your true Self and feel the inherent acceptance that lies within you that you will successfully become aware of all that you are, all that you can become, and all that you deserve.

I believe that last sentence is so important that it is worth repeating. It is when you find your true Self *and feel the inherent acceptance that lies within you* that you will successfully become aware of all that you are, all that you can become, and all that you deserve.

Personal Rulebook Play
MY SENSE OF SELF-WORTH

Get out your Personal Rulebook, and think about the level of respect you have for yourself. Do you accept yourself just as you are? Do you live and act in ways that set boundaries to support your personal self-worth? Write down your responses to the following questions in your rulebook.

- What could you do to create a more caring attitude for yourself?

- What could you stop doing that is sabotaging your ability to feel worthy of success and happiness?

- Who in your life supports your sense of self-respect and self-worth?

- Who does not?

- How can you protect or stand up for yourself by setting healthy boundaries around self-respect and self-worth?

Rule #3
DECIDE ON THE LOCATION OF HOME BASE

After determining who is IT and where the boundaries of the game are in the childhood game of Hide & Seek, the next rule is to decide on a location of home base. This is the place where every round begins. It is where the IT team keeps someone on guard at all times to protect the area once they have found those hiding. In your MASTERY game of Hide & Seek, your home base is also a key factor to your success.

While home base in your MASTERY game is not exactly a location in the physical sense of the word, it is located within you. It is your center, your core, and your safe zone. At this internal home base, there is always acceptance and worthiness. This is a place where you can go to find an inner knowing and peace that comes from being connected with your core. Think about a time when you felt completely at ease with your world. It may have been a time in nature or another moment when you were alone with yourself and all was well. There was no anxiety about tomorrow, no worries about yesterday, and just an acceptance of being present in that moment. These are examples of being at home base. These "connected" moments are times when you are able to get out of your head and into your heart. I don't mean getting "into your heart" in the sappy sense, but as a deep internal knowing that all is well.

This feeling of peace . . . of connection . . . of knowing comes from alignment. *Alignment* is defined as a position of agreement or alliance. This alignment is crucial to winning the MASTERY game of Hide & Seek. It is an alliance with your authentic Self, an agreement you make with that Self that says, "I got your back, no matter what." Knowing that you can always come back to home base where your teammate—*You*—is standing guard is how you remain strong and how you get recharged when you need to.

Let me share with you the pass key of the MASTERY game of Hide & Seek. The key that unlocks the door to success is all about this home-base rule. The key—or goal of the game—is to find *You* in every situation. *You* is always waiting at home base. Your part in the game is to enjoy exploring the boundaries of each game, and then end up at home base where *You* is patiently standing guard and waiting for you to return and align with all that you've learned and all that you long to become. The real *You* is constantly pointing you in the direction of authenticity. It's like a lighthouse beaming brightly for you to see through the storms. Your MASTERY games always lead to *You*.

> ### Personal Rulebook Play
> ## MY HOME BASE
>
> Grab your Personal Rulebook and think of a time when you were completely content and at peace, then respond to the following questions:
>
> ✦ What were you doing that led up to that feeling?
>
> ✦ What choices had you made that contributed to being in that place of alignment?
>
> ✦ How did those choices connect you to your home base? Your *You*?
>
> ✦ Do you remember being in your head and thinking a lot, or were you in your heart and present in that moment?
>
> ✦ How do you think your life would be if you were able to connect to that centered authentic place on a daily basis?

Rule #4
OLLY OLLY OXEN FREE

The fourth rule in Hide & Seek is to acknowledge "Olly Olly Oxen Free." In the childhood game, this term has three meanings. Each of these relates to the MASTERY game of Hide & Seek as well. In the childhood game it means:

✦ Players can come out from hiding without losing the game.

✦ The position of the sides has changed. (Offense to defense, goals change to the other side of the field, etc.)

✦ All who are "out" can come back in without penalty.

The meanings for each of the above as they relate to becoming a master are your lifelines, your "mulligans," your do-overs, or your get-out-of-jail-free cards. They go a little something like this:

Players can come out from hiding without losing the game.
Don't be afraid to come out and try. This rule means that you can *always* call Olly Olly Oxen Free, so release the idea that if you try and fail, you will lose the game. Words teach us knowledge, but we learn most through experience. If you stay in your comfort zone and don't step out to experience something new or challenge yourself with something unknown, you will not feel the exhilaration that comes from taking that step of faith. Even if you try and fail, at a minimum you can be proud of the fact that you overcame your fear of trying! As my four-year-old son says, "If that doesn't work, try something else. And if that doesn't work, try something else. And if that doesn't work, try something else. And if that . . ." Success is not about the number of times you failed, it is about trying one more time than the number of times you failed.

The position of the sides has changed. (Offense to defense, goals change to the other side of the field, etc.)
As with any game, your MASTERY game of Hide & Seek will include some game changers—those moments when something major happens that creates a noticeable change in momentum. Life is always going to hand you a game-changing moment. It may be a simple pause in the game where teams are changing sides and you have to reorganize yourself to adjust to the new orientation. An example of that kind of game changer would be a reorganization at the company where you work. Or it may be a rule change where you have to go back to the drawing board and completely revamp your game plan (like if you were laid off). It could even be a player change where you need to take some time to determine who's in the game, who's out of the game, and go back to pick your team over again (like when a partner leaves a relationship).

Whatever the game changer may be, a successful team leader will accept it, make the change, and keep on playing. If you can follow this same formula, you, too, will successfully play your MASTERY games of Hide & Seek. Being able to embrace change in your life, even when it is not something you welcome, means going with the flow of life rather than resisting the very nature of life itself.

Part of becoming a master is knowing how to handle change. By nature, we are creatures of habit and change can often bring up feelings of fear or anxiety. Yet change is a universal principle that reflects the constant movement of our very existence, so the one thing you can count on is that things are going to change. It is inevitable.

To effectively handle change, it's necessary to apply your understanding of the "principle of movement" described earlier. Knowing how to balance the qualities of quietude and activity allows you to skillfully navigate those inevitable changes. As you play your MASTERY games of Hide & Seek, you will have opportunities to practice this combination of stillness and activity. There will be times during your games when you will want to be quiet and alert, and other times when you will want to sprint. It is up to you to listen for the cues from within to know which stance you need to take at any given moment.

In most games, when there is fear or anxiety, you want to first be very still so you can assess the situation. You may then decide to run once you know there is an actual threat. This is a helpful practice to remember next time you feel fear or anxiety. Stop and take time to ask yourself, "What is it, exactly, that is causing me to feel this way?" You may discover it is simply your own mind playing tricks on you, or you may discover there is something wrong with the situation and your intuition is flashing the warning signal. ("RUN!")

Just as Olly Olly Oxen Free has a natural optimism to it, during any time of contemplation, you also have the choice to pick change that is positive, abundant, and fortunate. When you make choices that allow you to grow and evolve, you nurture and support yourself, which leads to comfort during times of uncertainty and unrest. The principle of change is about movement. Mastering this principle means knowing when to be still and when to take action.

All who are "out" can come back in without penalty.

The game of life is not a game of "three outs and you're gone." You can always get back in the game. Sometimes, you just need to be at home base to get centered and regain your footing before you get back in the game. There is a lesson in every experience, and when you take time to reflect on your setbacks or failures, you recharge your internal batteries for what is next to come. I have heard many successful people say, "There is no failure as long as you learn something from it." They say it because they know that their success is the result of lessons learned from many failed attempts. Having this belief will give you the freedom to say, "Why not try?" rather than stay in your comfort zone and wonder what could have been.

When is the last time you heard Olly Olly Oxen Free? I hope it brings a smile to your face as it takes you back to your childhood games of Hide & Seek. Go ahead, shout out "Olly Olly Oxen Free!" next time you feel like you've failed. If you actually shout it at the top of your lungs it will most likely make you giggle; that alone will help put you in a new state—physically and mentally—so that you can change your focus from the feeling of failure to the pondering of what can be learned.

Personal Rulebook Play
TIME TO CALL "OLLY OLLY OXEN FREE"

Grab your Personal Rulebook and think about how can you use Olly Olly Oxen Free in your life right now. Then answer the following questions:

+ Do you need a time-out?

+ Do you need permission to just go for it?

+ How do you deal with change?

+ Do you know when to be still and alert in order to listen to your gut feeling?

+ Do you ask others for their opinion or do you trust yourself and your intuition?

+ Do you need to release a feeling of self-condemnation for a failure and be grateful for the lesson in the experience?

+ Do you believe that there is, or can be, a lesson in every situation?

+ If so, what is the lesson you can learn from a current "failure" in your life right now?

This current situation doesn't have to be a big failure. It could be something as simple as the way you handled a conversation with your partner. Without judgment or guilt, think about what you could have done differently or what awareness you now have because of the situation. And then . . . call, "Olly Olly Oxen Free!"

Rule #5
START COUNTING AND . . . "GAME ON!"

The final rule is to start counting and begin the game. This is where all the juice of the journey gets tasty. It is the moment of excitement as everyone runs to find their hiding place. It is the time when those who are IT anxiously await the end of their count so they can start to explore. It is your moment to eagerly anticipate the journey to discover all that you are and to embrace the experience.

An odyssey—it is a long and eventful or adventurous journey or experience. So start counting! Enjoy the excitement of the adventure. Savor the journey. Embrace the winding road. Discover the awe. This MASTERY game of Hide & Seek is your personal odyssey!

CHAPTER THREE

How to Play the Game

*N*ow that you know the rules, let's dive into more practical ways you can play your MASTERY games of Hide & Seek. While a concept is a great tool and a metaphor helps you to grasp the concept, they don't always go far in helping you implement the actual experience in your life. And remember, we learn through experience. Throughout the remainder of *Hide & Seek,* we will explore four areas of the MASTERY game of Hide & Seek to help you make it practical in your life. Each area is represented by one of four parts in the book.

Part One is Learning the Game. You may be thinking, *Didn't we just do that?* Nope. We just learned the rules of the game. Learning how to strategically play the game is a whole different story.

Learning the Game consists of two parts of the MASTERY acronym: *M* for *Maximize Your Impact* and *A* for *Achieve through Alignment.* Seeing how this game applies to you personally, while knowing how to use it to your fullest advantage, is the goal of Maximizing Your Impact. In addition, you will learn how to create the life you want rather than feeling like life is happening to you in Achieve through Alignment. The characteristic of alignment is the basis of all achievement. When you learn how to align with *You,* life will take on a whole new perspective.

Part Two is Discovering Your Truth. It is also represents two parts of the MASTERY acronym: *S* for *Savor the Journey* and *T* for *Think with Compassion*. Within Discovering Your Truth, you will find ways to connect with what is true for you. We are all unique, yet there are consistent elements in life that we each possess—and need—in order to attain a level of mastery in our lives.

By understanding the importance of these elements, and learning to apply processes that allow you to be present and have more awareness, you will realize the potential of fulfillment that can come from every aspect of your experience. This ability to realize your potential for fulfillment is the outcome of Savor the Journey. Additionally, Think with Compassion will show you how to integrate the polar opposites that lie within each and every one of us. Seeing the interplay of the masculine and feminine roles, and grasping the ability to live from your head *and* your heart, creates a dynamic power that each—on their own—cannot produce.

Part Three is Finding the Balance. This part of the MASTERY acronym includes *E* for *Engage with Integrity* and *R* for *Retreat for Sanity*. Balance is the key to continued success, and within Finding the Balance, you will learn what takes you out of balance and how to restore it.

By knowing the way life flows and your ability to go with the flow through an authentic approach, you will learn how to Engage with Integrity. This ability to actively engage is then balanced with the ability to retreat and appreciate the power in stillness. Retreat for Sanity will help you to become a master by truly understanding how to effectively nurture yourself mentally, emotionally, spiritually, and physically.

Part Four is Ready or Not, Here I Come! The final part of the MASTERY acronym is *Y* for *You Are the Key*. This final piece of the puzzle is the exclamation point that fuels all of the other areas. Learning how you connect with your authentic Self is the key that unlocks the door to unlimited success and boundless joy in your life. You Are the Key will set you on your way, saying, "Ready or not, here I come!"

It is important to note that as we move into the MASTERY games, we address the underlying question central to all human actions. What do we want, and why do we want it? If you ask someone the question, "What do you want most in the world?" And then you ask them, "Why do you want it?" The bottom-line answer is always, "Because it will make me feel happy."

For example, when someone says she wants to have a family more than anything in the world, why does she want that? Because a family will give her the experience of being a parent and raising children. Why does she want to be a parent? Because it will give her a sense of purpose. Why does she want purpose? Because it will give her a feeling of fulfillment. Why does she want to feel fulfillment? Because she believes it will make her feel happy.

But *happy* is not the best word to describe this ultimate feeling we are talking about here. Happy actually comes from your external surroundings and is fleeting. *Joy* would be a better choice, and *joy* is the word we will use throughout the rest of our exploration into the MASTERY game of Hide & Seek. Joy is a genuine contentment that comes from deep within your being and is sustainable.

As you go through the practical applications of the MASTERY game of Hide & Seek, remember that every tool, every process, and every idea that resonates with you is designed to help you discover the answers to your underlying question: What do you want and why do you want it? If you can begin to shift your thinking to understand that the reason you want to be successful in business, for example, is because you want to feel a profound contentment, it will help you to see your desires in a different light.

This is not to discount the fact that part of what you want may be money, recognition, and challenges. Those are all great goals, which can be a very fun part of your life experience. However, understanding that they simply represent the external evidence of happiness and that happiness is fleeting will help you enjoy them for what they are rather than using them to reflect who you are. This is so important that I want to say it again in a different way: Allowing external evidence to become the basis of who you believe you are will always leave you feeling empty and unfulfilled. What I invite you to discover is the authentic desire within you that brings you true joy. When you do this, you will be able to enjoy the external evidence, while savoring the internal joy that springs from your need to experience and follow whatever is most meaningful and significant to you.

PART ONE

LEARNING
THE GAME

CHAPTER FOUR

MAXIMIZE YOUR IMPACT

M stands for *Maximize Your Impact.* This characteristic in the MASTERY game of Hide & Seek will mean different things to different people. If you are competitive, you will see maximizing your impact as the way to win. If you are focused on how you can grow as an individual, you will see maximizing your impact as a way to become more self-actualized. If you are analytical, you will want to know the facts and see how they can be applied to your life in a practical manner. One of my favorite discoveries has been realizing that we all see the world through different lenses, and there is no right or wrong way to play the game.

Becoming a master and maximizing your impact is all about understanding what you really want in your life, and how to use your natural tendencies and gifts to create consistent and sustainable satisfaction. If you don't know what it is you want, you will not be able to build momentum in your life. Momentum is what allows you to make an impact. The way we each maximize our impact will be as unique as each of us. Nevertheless, there are six steps you can take (in your own unique way, of course) to maximize your impact:

Step 1: Clarity of Desire and Steady Determination

Step 2: True Power

Step 3: Integration

Step 4: Transformation

Step 5: Manifestation

Step 6: Hitting the Bull's-Eye

Let's take a look at each of these steps in turn.

Step 1 CLARITY OF DESIRE AND STEADY DETERMINATION

Learning to maximize your impact is really about figuring out how to make the most of your life. We can make that a little less intimidating by breaking it down to making the most of your day . . . or your hour . . . or this moment. There is no right or wrong way to do it; it just takes clarity of desire and steady determination. Clarity of desire means knowing what you want your impact to be. Studies have shown that the working population spends the majority of time being reactive during the workday. Most people spend their time reacting to what's happening, like responding to emails, being drawn into a conversation, or answering queries from clients or colleagues. These are all ways we stay busy, but we are not consciously choosing how to be productive. From my personal experience with clients, I think it is safe to say most people spend the majority of their lives being reactive at home as well as at the office.

Being reactive is part of life; important and urgent things are bound to come up during the day, but clarity of desire helps us guide the majority of our day toward the outcomes that are most important to us. How many times have you started your day with great intentions only to have it derailed with unexpected family or work demands? For me, there have been too many to count, and what I have noticed on those days is that I tend to feel more stressed, frustrated, and impatient. Through my lens, one part of maximizing my impact means getting things done that matter to me. When I pro-actively spend most of my day doing things that I love—and that are important to me—I feel content and fulfilled. I believe most of us feel this same way, although what is important to each of us can look very different.

If managing a multimillion-dollar company is what you really love doing, then you will be fulfilled by all of the challenges that come along with that job. If raising children to become responsible, loving, and authentic adults is what you really love doing, then you will also be ful-filled by the many challenges that come along with that job. If giving back to others or caring for animals who have been abused is what you desire deep down, then part of maximizing your impact means taking part in organizations that focus on those mutual passions.

Personal Rulebook Play
MY DEFINITION OF *IMPACT*

Let's first define what *impact* means to you. Pull out your Personal Rulebook and write down your answers to these questions:

✦ What are the three most important things you desire to have in your life?

✦ Why are they important to you?

✦ What is stopping you from having these things in your life?

Once you have finished reading this chapter and have done all of its Plays, we will come back to this Rulebook Play and use the con-cepts to complete your game plan.

Clarity of desire and steady determination make up the first step in the Maximize Your Impact part of your MASTERY games of Hide & Seek. Getting clarity may require you to do some "soul searching" in order to find what is truly meaningful to you. Knowing what is meaningful to you *is* the foundation to making an impact. When you take the time to dig deep and discover what is meaningful in your life, you will find your days are affected in a really powerful way. You will feel clear-minded with little confusion, and it will initiate a drive within you to take action.

In addition to clarity of desire, the other part of this step is steady determination. To win any game, it requires practice. Teams don't win championships by just casually putting together a group of people and heading onto the field. At a minimum, winning requires a leader, a carefully chosen team, a strategic game plan, a hunger to be the best one can be, interactive coaching, and lots of practice.

This is what steady determination looks like. It is you becoming the leader of your life, choosing the teammates or coaches you want to help you, coming up with a game plan, having a hunger within you to be the best you can possibly be, and practicing. Practicing is the practical application of steady determination. It is knowing the outcome and consistently practicing the activities to reach your goal. It is creating rituals and habits that will support your desired outcome. It may mean practicing self-acceptance so you can begin to appreciate your value and self-worth, practicing your communication skills so you can advance your career, or practicing speaking your true feelings so you can create intimacy in your personal relationships. Whatever it is, this steady determination will allow you to increase your performance at a sustainable rate.

Step 2   TRUE POWER

The second step toward maximizing your impact is to grasp the enormity of your true power. *Power* is defined as the ability to do something or act in a particular way. This sounds like such a minimal definition compared to the *enormity* of your true power, as stated above. True power in the MASTERY game of Hide & Seek is the power of God within each one of us. In Hollywood terms, it is the Force that Yoda taught Luke to harness to become a Jedi. In the real world, it is the Life Force within you that has the power to create the Universe.

Let me take a moment to address something. The purpose of your Hide & Seek games is to playfully take you on a journey of self-discovery. Throughout these pages, you are going to hear me talk about the most profound part of self-discovery—the spiritual component. I know there are lots of religious and spiritual perspectives out there, and I think everyone has the right to their own beliefs. Ninety-eight percent of Americans believe in God. Therefore, so we can all get as much from the lessons of MASTERY as possible, I am going to use the term *God*. I will also frequently use the terms *true Self* and *You* to describe the nonphysical, awe-inspiring part of you—your Soul.

Now that you see the scope I am reaching for here, let's see how we can make this practical in your everyday life. You hold the power of your experience. While you cannot always control what happens in your life, you can control *how you react* to what happens in your life. Your true power is in the choices you make every moment of every day. Your true power is in every cell of your being and at your disposal whenever you need it. Your true power is in your ability to find the *You* that is hiding during any circumstance and connect with it.

You hold the power of your experience.

How do you connect with it? One way is to learn to trust your gut. Whether you call this a hunch or intuition, we are all born with the ability to use this sixth sense to affect the course of our lives. I believe one of the most powerful innate tools we have is our intuition. If you are someone who relies on facts and doesn't give much credit to this "out there" intuition stuff, stay with me for a moment. You can logically work your way through the following explanation to see how to apply your innate gifts for analyzing the facts and then determine if it will work for you.

Many times we ignore the subtle hints telling us to change course or move full speed ahead. Why? It can be a number of things, but here are just a few reasons:

- **Lack of Attention:** We are so busy thinking about the infinite to-dos on our list that we just don't take the time to stop and listen.

- **Lack of Confidence:** We question our gut feeling, or try to "logic" our way around it.

- **Denial:** We hear it, but don't want it to be true. We don't think we are ready for whatever change may need to happen.

- **Outside Influences:** We listen to others and follow their counsel rather than trusting our gut.

These are each examples of how we give away our true power. Yet when you stand in your power and believe in your ability to direct your life, there is *nothing* that can stop you. I mean that, literally. You will find that as you begin to believe in your ability to accomplish whatever you set your mind to, connecting to your innate power will get easier and easier. With clarity of your desire and steady determination as your foundation, you can begin to tap into a source of unlimited energy that will be the fuel needed to maximize your impact.

This unlimited energy is what gives you whatever you need to accomplish your desire and make your mark. For the researcher who wants to make an impact on the world by finding a cure, this true power is the longing to continue searching for answers through hours of calculations and endless studies. For the teacher who wants to make an impact by guiding children and helping them believe in their self-worth, it is the drive that allows them to nurture each child beyond the curriculum in the classroom. For the inventor who wants to impact the world with the next innovation that will change the way we live, it is the unending flow of creative energy that brings forth idea after idea and an insatiable thirst to never give up.

How do you connect to this power in practical ways? Through deliberate intention. For example, take the four preceding reasons we ignore our intuition. By staying aware of them, you can begin to tap into your true power. You can make the following choices instead:

- ❖ **Lack of Attention:** Take the time to stop and listen. Pay attention to the "signs" or coincidences that are happening around you. Once you have clarity about your desires, put your focus there.

- ❖ **Lack of Confidence:** We build confidence through trust. Begin to trust yourself as you go through your day. If doing this is new to you, start with little things. It could be as simple as making a decision and then telling yourself that it was a good one. At the end of your day, go through the things you did, and write down your "good choices." This is just one example of how you can build confidence. Focus on the positive things you have done and try not to spend time feeling guilty, or bad, about something you think you could have done better. Remember, *confidence* comes from the root word *confide,* and this is your opportunity to confide in yourself.

- ❖ **Denial:** Whether you are ready or not, reality is always playing with you in the present moment. Rather than denying what is, consider taking a closer look at what is, and then direct your focus on how you want to move into the future (which is really just the next present moment reality, right?). One of the Hide & Seek rules says it best: "Ready or not, here I come!"

✦ **Outside Influences:** Just as you learn to build confidence by confiding in yourself, you can build great trust and tap into your true power by practicing *not* giving your power away. Listening to others to hear a different perspective can be a huge help in your life, as long as it is only one part of your process. When you deliberately focus on being the final say in any decision for yourself, you are connecting with your true power.

Personal Rulebook Play
TAPPING INTO MY TRUE POWER

With each example above, you can see how your deliberate and intentional focus upon your own intuition is one of the best ways to live from a new perspective. Take out your Personal Rulebook and answer the following questions:

✦ How can I tap into my true power?

✦ Is there an area in my life where I am not playing all-out?

✦ What am I doing that is giving away my power?

✦ What are three things I could do to start standing in my own power?

Each time you access your true power, you are actually finding the *You* in your MASTERY games of Hide & Seek. *You* is where this power resides, and remember, finding *You* is the whole point of the game. Can you see how profound the "game" actually is? As you continue through the MASTERY games, I hope you will begin to feel the grandness of this "game." While games can be fun, lighthearted, and exciting, they can also be heartfelt, intense, and profound.

I'd like to give you one final nugget before we move on to the next step to maximize your impact. Here is an affirmation that you can use to remind yourself that you are in charge, and *You* (your Soul, your connection to God) are the source of your true power: *I hold the power of my experience.* You can repeat this affirmation to yourself when you wake up, when you go to bed, when you are in a situation where you feel helpless, or when you want to reinforce a feeling of success. Affirmations are a great way to connect to your true power. The key when using an affirmation is to "feel" what you are saying. If you say, "I am the creator of my reality," but feel like "that kind of luck happens to other people, not me," it will be difficult to see the results in your life. We will go into more detail and practical advice on this in Chapter 5: Achieve through Alignment.

Step 3   INTEGRATION

As I've said more than once already, experience teaches. When you are able to bring together the information you've learned intellectually with the actions you take, you make huge leaps toward maximizing your impact. Integration is knowledge immersed in experience. When you integrate something, you change who you are forever. Your actions become influenced by your thoughts, and your thoughts become influenced by your actions.

Integration is knowledge immersed in experience.

The first time I heard the word *integration,* I didn't really get what it meant. I just had a hard time wrapping my mind around the word. Funny that it would be difficult for the mind to understand "experience," isn't it? Actually, it makes perfect sense. Our mind is designed to logically think through a situation. Our mind does the analysis. It calculates what is happening, but it doesn't "experience" the situation. This "experiencing" is happening in another part of our being. We could say our heart is where we experience a situation. And our heart is where integration takes place, at least on the physical level. Part of mastering your Hide & Seek games is understanding that integration is multidimensional. Integration happens on the emotional, mental, physical, and spiritual levels. Integration within the MASTERY game of Hide & Seek is being able to find the different aspects of *You* that may be hiding.

As explained in Chapter 2: The Rules, there is not necessarily a physical location of home base, and neither are there specific locations in your body for the different aspects of you. According to the *Collected Works of CG Jung: Archetypes and the Collective Unconscious,* Jung discussed the concept of archetypes and believed them to be "psychophysical patterns existing in the universe, given specific expression by human consciousness and culture." Jung also proposed that each archetype had a dual nature: "Each exists both in the psyche and in the world at large."

Basically, archetypes are aspects of your true Self. Think of an archetype as a part of you that represents a certain characteristic of who you are. For example, you are a mom or a dad, a businessperson or a socialite, a leader or a follower. These are all examples of archetypes. They are part of you, and as Jung also stated, they are also part of others. These archetypes are not just owned by individuals. They are within individuals and also represent distinct energies on their own within the collective consciousness. For example, using the archetype of "leader," you can probably think of someone you know who is a leader. That person has certain qualities you are able to observe that make him or her a leader in your eyes. Now think about those qualities without a particular person attached. There are certain aspects— or qualities—that create the energy of a leader. This energy is the leader archetype. That expressive energy is what I am referring to when I reference an archetype in the MASTERY game of Hide & Seek.

To maximize your impact, you are constantly connecting to the energies of different archetypes within the MASTERY games. In every game, or life situation, you have the ability to draw on different aspects of yourself to win. Winning is choosing the aspect that allows you to connect with your authentic Self. For example, if you are heading into a business meeting, you may be calling on—or connecting with—your leader archetype and/or your salesperson archetype. These are aspects of yourself that will help you be successful in your current situation or game.

To truly become a master, though, we have to take a deeper look at archetypes. Archetypes are not just the roles we play in our society. They go much deeper and reside in the different dimensions of our lives. As we have discussed, archetypes are present on all four levels— the physical, emotional, mental, and spiritual levels.

At a deeper level, archetypes can be represented by words such as: the Sage, the Visionary, the Hero, the Warrior, the Healer, the Queen, the Knight, the Lover, the Nurturer, and so on. These archetypes almost have a personality of their own, don't they? Yet, as you think about each of them, you can most likely connect with at least a few of their aspects within yourself.

Personal Rulebook Play
CONNECTING WITH MY ARCHETYPES

Get out your Personal Rulebook. In this Play, you are going to learn to connect with your own archetypes. You will be using the power of your voice for this activity, but feel free to jot down any notes or ideas that come to you in your rulebook. Think about a situation in your life that may be causing you to feel uncertainty. Use the following archetype process to gain more clarity.

First, think about the question(s) you have concerning this situation. One of your questions might be "How do I handle this situation?" Then read the following archetype descriptions:

✦ **The King or Queen:** This aspect is the confident leader, the one willing to make the tough decisions, the one with a sureness of will and meaningful purpose.

✦ **The Warrior:** This aspect is the brave fighter, the one willing to take on the challenge, the one with a courageous, bold, and fearless spirit.

✦ **The Lover:** This aspect is the passionate enthusiast, the one with a zest for life, the one with deep affection, tenderness, and a yearning for connection.

✦ **The Sage:** This aspect is the wise guru, the one who understands the conundrums of life, the one who knows all answers and expresses them in sensible, clever, and perceptive ways.

Now, see if you can connect with each of these archetypes within you and ask yourself how each would answer your question. As you go through each archetype, complete each of the following statements out loud with the *first thing* that comes to your mind. Complete the statement at least four times for each archetype.

The King/Queen says, _____.

The Warrior says, _____.

The Lover says, _____.

The Sage says, _____.

If you're having trouble connecting to the archetype, touch the place on your body where you feel the archetype resides. For example, you may feel the Lover resides in your heart. Tap on your heart while you are completing the above statement for the Lover.

Have fun with this process! You can even call on your "Smarty-Pants" archetype to answer questions for you when you feel the need to lighten up.

STEP 4 TRANSFORMATION

A beautiful thing begins to happen once you have clarity of desire and you develop consistency through steady determination. You are able to tune in to your true power.

You begin to integrate the different aspects of your true Self—the *You* in your MASTERY game—into your life.

As a kid, did you ever learn about the process of how a caterpillar turns into a butterfly? When I was a youngster in school we had a glass aquarium where we were able to actually watch the process unfold. It was amazing to watch this little soft and fuzzy creature form into a chrysalis, and then eventually break through it to reveal a gorgeous winged butterfly—a creature then able to experience the world from a whole new perspective.

This is what each of us does as we play our MASTERY games of Hide & Seek. As we begin each game, we have a perspective that is very different from the one we have after we have discovered all of the wonders of our existence through our experiences. At first, it's as though we get to see the world from the caterpillar's perspective as we slowly make our way around. It is a smaller perspective. It's a way to see some possibilities that are right in front of us or close to where we reside. We get to taste the sweetness of life, just as the caterpillar tastes the sweetness of the host plant it consumes. We get to learn how to blend in with our surroundings, just as the caterpillar blends into its surroundings. We get to take on grand challenges, just as the caterpillar does when he is at the bottom of a forty-foot tree about to make the climb.

And just as the caterpillar is on its odyssey, we, too, are going through the process of transformation as we travel on our journey. This transformation is a natural part of life. It is instinctual. We each get to choose—whether we do it consciously or not—the path and speed of our transformation. We are here to experience life in whatever way we choose. We each get to choose our path, and I think that's one of the most invigorating parts of life. You can choose to live a life of simplicity or chaos. You can choose to live for love or drama. You can choose to focus on proactively creating your adventure or to just react to whatever life brings you. There is no right or wrong way to live your life. It's *your* adventure . . . *your* odyssey.

Just as the caterpillar is on its odyssey, we, too, are going through the process of transformation as we travel on our journey.

The path of transformation is a unique and very personal experience. Just as the caterpillar goes inward to undergo its transformation, we, too, must go inward to create transformation. Our chrysalises are made up of emotions, thoughts, experiences, and space. Our emotions, thoughts, and experiences reflect our perspective. Space gives us the empty silence to listen to our inner wisdom and hear God. It's through this process of quiet inner reflection that true transformation takes place.

Transformation. It sounds like a pretty big change doesn't it? But for you to transform, it doesn't have to mean the heavens open up and you hear angels singing. (Insert the *Ahhhhhh* in your mind to get the full effect of that visual!) Have you ever said, "Just give me a minute," so that you could figure out what you wanted to do? This is one way you give yourself the space to connect and go inward, gain a little perspective, and sort through your thoughts. And through this simple process of going inward, you are creating opportunities for transformations in your life. While many of these moments may be small and simple, it is the act of going inward, consistently, that creates transformation.

Transformation can also look like a twenty-car train wreck where your entire world has been derailed and you have to sift through a messy disaster as you pick up the pieces. This process is challenging, sometimes to the point where you think you may break. Yet you make it through, and you are stronger, wiser, and happier than ever before. The most challenging times are the ones that bring forth your greatest strength. And just as the caterpillar breaks through its chrysalis to emerge as a completely transformed and beautiful butterfly, you break through, too, and have the potential to become a more beautiful . . . you.

Did you know that a butterfly must also break through the chrysalis on its own without help or its wings will be too weak, and it will die? The same is true with your transformation. Others cannot do the inner work that is required to transform. Only you can do that work. That's why you are "IT" in your MASTERY games of Hide & Seek. Only you can walk your path, find your true Self, and grow into the multicolored butterfly that is uniquely you.

So let me ask you a question: Once the transformation has occurred, is the butterfly still the caterpillar? Are you still . . . you?

Of course you are! You are absolutely still *You*. In fact, you are more *You* than you have ever been before. As you break through your chrysalis, you have been through a transformation. And just as the caterpillar is now able to fly and see the world from a new perspective, you, too, have the ability to experience life from a new vantage point. And unlike the caterpillar, who experiences this transformation only once during its lifetime, you get to do it over and over again during your lifetime. Every MASTERY game can have some form of transformation in it. While the major transformations may seem more remarkable, it is the little transformations that happen along your journey that lead up to those so-called remarkable ones.

Transformation is becoming more of who you already are. The *You* that is hiding in your MASTERY games of Hide & Seek is the full expression of all that is. The *You* that you seek during every situation in life is the authentic Self that lies deep within your being. This ability to transform into more of who you already are, and all that you are destined to become, is what gives you genuine, sustainable joy and fulfillment. Sustainable! Just as the butterfly does not turn back into the caterpillar, when you experience true transformation, you can't go back. And you don't want to go back. Your new perspective will be exhilarating, and your broader perspective will become your new normal. Then, eagerly, you'll begin the process all over again.

Personal Rulebook Play
MAKING SPACE FOR TRANSFORMATION

Get out your Personal Rulebook and think back to a time in your life when you remember feeling the exhilaration of a transformation—an "aha" moment that shifted the way you looked at something in your life. Was it an unexpected glimpse of enlightenment that rocked your world? Or was it a simple adjustment that sent you in a new direction on your path? Just as changing the angle you are walking by five degrees can lead you to an entirely different destination thousands of miles from your original journey's end, changing your perspective by a few degrees will also lead you to an entirely new conclusion. Now, think about the following questions and take notes in your rulebook:

✦ How can you proactively go inward to listen to the silence like the caterpillar? What are some specific methods that you gravitate toward when you "need a little space"?

✦ Are there ways that you can incorporate this process into your life to make space for transformation? Perhaps by working with a coach? Meditating? Reading books?

✦ What emotions, thoughts, and experiences are part of the chrysalis you are creating in your life right now?

✦ How do you think you and your life will look once you break through this current chrysalis?

✦ Can you see the importance of how this current chrysalis can help you create a level of transformation to become more authentic? How could you find more of the real *You* right now?

STEP 5   MANIFESTATION

Manifestation is defined as an event, action, or object that clearly shows or embodies something. Being able to see tangible evidence—or manifestations—in life is part of what makes your odyssey eventful and adventurous. Let's face it: manifestations make it interesting! To put it simply, manifesting means turning your thoughts into reality. Your life experience is the tangible evidence of what you choose to create through your focus and intention. What does that really mean? It means you actually have the ability to create whatever you want in your life.

To maximize our impact, we have to know how to manifest things in our life. These "things" may be emotions, experiences, objects, money, or people. The first step in maximizing your ability to manifest is to realize that you create your experience. This liberating concept alone has the power to shift your entire life almost instantly. I'm not kidding around when I say that when you make a decision to believe that you have the ability to choose what you want in life, it's like flipping the "on" switch of empowerment.

For some, this idea creates the question, "If I have the ability to create the life I want, then why am I struggling financially?" Or "Why don't I have the relationship I want?" Or "Why am I in a job that sucks?"

The answer lies in where you choose to put your focus. For example, with money, do you spend time thinking about how much money you *don't* have? Do you worry about not having enough money? Do you fear that money is scarce and you must hold on to what you've got?

As it relates to your relationship, are you afraid you'll never find your perfect mate? Do you wish your current partner were more or less of a given characteristic? Do you seem to choose partners who, along with you, create a common pattern of destruction?

And for that sucky job, what is it that you spend your time focused on? Is it all of the reasons you *don't* like your job? Is it talking about how you *don't* like your boss or coworkers? Do you look for opportunities to use your strengths to excel, or do you focus your attention on what drains you during your day?

All three of the above examples show the power of manifestation. If your attention and, more important, your emotions are aligned with the lack of what you want in life rather than with the abundance of what you want, your life will reflect one of lack. On the other hand, if you focus on abundance rather than lack, your life will be filled with financial, relationship, and professional abundance.

When you flip the "on" switch of empowerment by realizing you create your reality, you add a new element to your MASTERY games of Hide & Seek. That element is like having a flashlight in the dark. You begin to have the ability to see things that you couldn't see before. Manifesting means seeing something that may have been there before, but you had not yet shined your flashlight in its direction. Whether you call it "mind over matter," "believing is seeing," or simply "focusing on what you want versus what you don't want," your ability to maximize your impact, at home or work, is directly related to where you choose to focus your attention. We will go into more detail and describe processes to support you in manifesting in Chapter 5: Achieve through Alignment. For now, let's look at the basic manifesting principles.

To become a master manifestor, you must be able to recognize two types of manifestation: emotional and physical. The majority of people live their lives reacting to what they can see, hear, smell, taste, or touch. These are examples of physical manifesting and are what most consider "reality." A master manifestor understands that the first manifestation is emotional.

Remember the Life Force we talked about earlier—the Force your inner Yoda is teaching you to connect with? This God-like energy is actually measurable in scientific terms. It is an energy that resides in various frequencies and its power, or impact, can be measured through scientific instruments. From a manifesting perspective, it is powerful beyond measure. We each have the ability to tap into the unlimited power that creates worlds by finding and connecting with our authentic Self. This is the true power we explored earlier in Step 2 when we talked about trusting your gut, intuition, or sixth sense.

To help make this emotional link more personal, think about the last time you felt really good, or . . . maybe a time you felt really bad. Did you feel confident? Did you feel clarity? Did you feel like you were being true to who you are and what you want? Certain emotional states are consistent with what we call feeling good or feeling bad, and your understanding of how they reveal your energetic frequency is very important to your success in life. When you are able to recognize the energy you are putting out emotionally, you will be able to see how the physical manifestations in your life match it. For example, feeling creative and inspired is associated with feeling good. Feeling tired and rundown is associated with feeling bad. This is how you can recognize emotional manifestations—by the way you feel.

Physical manifestation, positive or negative, comes after you have focused your intention and created emotion around your desire. Let me once again clarify an important point here: If your focused desire is about the lack of something, you're creating emotion and energy that will manifest more of the lack. This is such an important under-standing and will mean the difference between maximizing your impact and feeling that you've fallen short. As you become more aware of this concept and deliberately choose where you want to focus your attention, you will be able to consciously choose the emotional state you live in, which will in turn create physical manifestations. You will literally be able to turn your thoughts into reality.

Over the past two decades, I have been learning how to focus my attention on finding and connecting with my inner Self—my *You* that is hiding in my MASTERY games of Hide & Seek. In doing so, I've learned to recognize the daily opportunities to feel the power I have to create and manifest anything in my life. This can be a positive emotional energy or negative emotional energy, each with equal abil-ity to attract more of the same. For example, sometimes I'm grumpy, frustrated, and irritable, which manifests things like an argument with my husband, snapping at my kids, or making a mistake at work.

I remember a day at work recently when I was choosing to focus on a situation where a coworker was negatively impacting my office. This individual was very rude to my assistant, and I was just sick of it. I chose to spend time talking about the situation with my assistant and then dwelling on the many similar past incidents of rudeness until I got myself all amped up about it.

Driving home, I felt so irritated by the situation. But at the same time, I was able to observe myself *in* the irritation and recognize that my choice of focus was not serving me, my assistant, the other coworker, or what I wanted to feel and experience in my life. This ability to be *in* an experience *and* at the same time be able to *observe* and have awareness *in the moment* is something that I chose to develop many years ago. In the beginning when I first learned about this con-cept, I even remember thinking, *I want to do that. I want to catch myself and become aware while it's happening, rather than realizing it later. If I can stop myself in the act, I can break old habits or destructive patterns and have a growth opportunity.*

We all have the ability to do this. When we can catch ourselves in the moment, we can choose to shift our attention back to creating the life we want rather than living reactively and creating a life we don't want. The day I spent focusing on the rude coworker caused me to manifest several unnecessary hassles (like spilling a box of cards and envelopes all over the driveway) before I clued in to the fact that my emotional perspective was just creating more situations that reflected it.

Here's the bottom line: the energy we put out is the energy we get back in return. The way you know what kind of energy you are putting out is by the way you feel. If you feel good, great, exhilarated, energized, and joyful, you are going to have a life filled with good, great, exhila-rating, energizing, and joyful people, places, and things. If you feel bummed, frustrated, irritated, bored, and unfulfilled, you will create a life of frustration, irritation, boredom, and nonfulfillment. I know it may sound too simple, but try it for yourself for a few days, weeks, months, or years. You'll see the results. And more important, you'll discover the power you have to maximize your impact through your ability to actualize your desires emotionally and physically in your life.

Personal Rulebook Play
WHAT AM I MANIFESTING?

Grab your Personal Rulebook. Take a moment to think about your day today. What kind of emotions were you feeling during the day? How did you spend your time? Where did you focus your attention? Write down your answers in your rulebook. Then, reflect on the following questions and add them to this Play:

✦ Are you able to see connections between the thoughts and emotions you were feeling and the circumstances or happenings in your day?

✦ If you were unhappy, stressed, or frustrated, can you think of ways you could have redirected your focus?

✦ Is there a habitual emotion that you spend the majority of your time feeling? What is that emotion? Joy? Excitement? Frustration? Anger? Depression? Unworthiness? Think about how feeling that emotion has affected your personal and/or professional success. Is it serving you in a positive way?

✦ What emotions would you *like* to start spending the majority of your time feeling? And how can you remind yourself to start putting more attention there throughout your day? You could read daily from an influential book, say affirmations each morning about how you want to feel, put random reminders on your phone, or even show a trusted friend or coworker how they could help you recognize when you are in a particular emotional pattern that's not serving you. Find a reminder or a few reminders that work for you.

The energy we put out is the energy we get back in return.

STEP 6: HITTING THE BULL'S-EYE

The final step in Maximizing Your Impact is hitting the bull's-eye. When an archery master lines up an arrow, where do you think he or she is looking? At the bull's-eye, right? It is highly unlikely that he or she would become a master by focusing attention anywhere other than on the center of the target. The same is true for us as we go through life and play our MASTERY games. Looking at our target—whatever it may be—during any given moment helps us zero in on our goals and desires and helps us line up our aim.

You get to choose what your target is, and there are endless targets you can choose. Hitting the bull's-eye applies to all areas of life— mental, emotional, spiritual, physical, and even financial. You profit, benefit, and gain when you aim at a specific and narrow target. The reason we are constantly learning about the importance of setting goals is because we progress toward our goals when we know where we are headed. We build momentum when we lean in one direction.

Knowing the bull's-eye and hitting the bull's-eye are two different things. When you get clarity about your desire, you decide what the target is and take aim. Hitting the bull's-eye requires skills, practice, and patience. It means overcoming pressure, releasing resistance, and keeping outside influences at bay. In real-life terms this may mean learning a new skill. It may mean being willing to step back from a stressful situation and look at your part in the problem, as well as your contribution to the solution. It may mean trying or testing something over and over again until you get it just right.

In the MASTERY game of Hide & Seek, *You* are the primary target of every game. Find your true Self, and hit the bull's-eye. If you are aiming at another target in that same game (aka situation) such as desiring a successful career, it looks like this: Once you have found *You* (hit the first target), you feel connected with your ability to succeed. It is then a process of discovering how you can use your innate talents and natural gifts to create success in your career (hitting the second target).

For instance, if you are really great at making people feel at ease, use that gift to build strong relationships. Leverage those relationships by looking at how, together, you can create win-win situations for everyone involved. If your innate gift is being able to see the pitfalls in a situation, put yourself in a position to offer help during planning processes, or look for ways to be involved in development. You can support the company's objectives in a very positive way by contributing insights that could potentially save a lot of time and money, which will potentially bring you more recognition, success, and money, too.

These are practical ways that you can aim at your target, hone your skills, and hit the bull's-eye. When you can aim at your target and consistently hit it, you have reached the level of mastery. The key is to remember that the first target is always to find your true Self. Once you find *You,* then it becomes easier to hit all of the other targets. It's like putting on a pair of glasses to see your target with 20/20 vision.

Personal Rulebook Play
HITTING THE BULL'S-EYE

Get out your Personal Rulebook, and think about your answers to the following questions. Then write down your thoughts under the heading for this Play.

✦ What targets are important in your life right now? Relationship? Career? Financial? Spiritual? Personal growth? Notice these may be the same as the three things you wrote down in your Personal Rulebook Play at the beginning of this chapter (wink, wink).

♦ What specifically do you want to *feel* when you hit the bull's-eye of each target? Remember, feeling is the first manifestation, which leads to the physical manifestation. Knowing how you want to feel—and beginning to imagine, visualize, and have a sense of what it will be like when you actually see the results—will initiate and escalate the momentum of your arrow.

♦ What skills do you need to perfect to become a master archer for each of your targets? Do you need to increase your sales skills for your career? Do you need to lighten up and have more fun in your relationship? Do you need to start believing there is an abundance of money out there, and decide you want to be a part of the natural flow of giving and receiving?

BRINGING IT ALL TOGETHER

As we've discussed, one of the surefire ways to find the success you long for in life is to find your true Self and live in authenticity. This authenticity allows you the freedom to just be you! There is nothing that can give us a greater sense of joy than being content and feeling happy with who we are. This sense of inner peace liberates us and allows us to experience life from a brave and open perspective.

There is nothing that can give us a greater sense of joy than being content and feeling happy with who we are.

Consistent and sustainable satisfaction . . . that *is* the target. Remember the ultimate answer to why we do what we do: We all just want to feel happy and content. When you master the six steps described in this chapter, you win over and over again.

You win because your life becomes what you want it to be. You win because you feel "at home" in your own skin. You win because you embrace and utilize your natural tendencies and gifts. This MASTERY game of Hide & Seek is all about you personally knowing how to find who you are. Maximizing Your Impact is applying these six steps to your life and using them to your fullest advantage in every game.

It looks a little something like this:

✦ You set your sights on what you want in your life, and don't let anything distract you from your outcome (Clarity of Desire and Steady Determination).

✦ You use your innate talents and gifts by bringing them into every part of your life (True Power and Integration).

✦ You grow as a person by looking inward while experiencing challenges and successes (Transformation).

✦ You use the knowledge and experience of feeling connected to your authentic Self to begin deliberately creating the emotional and physical life you crave (Manifestation).

✦ You bring that ability to manifest anything you want in your life together with skill and focused practice—be it mentally, emotionally, spiritually, physically, and financially (Hitting the Bull's-Eye).

Get creative! There are endless ways and games for you to find your true Self and take yourself to the highest level of personal and professional success you desire. Now that you have the intellectual understanding of these six steps, it is time to make it real by applying it to your life. Let's go back to that Personal Rulebook Play we started at the beginning of this chapter and look at how you can apply these six steps to help you maximize your personal impact.

Personal Rulebook Playback
DEFINING WHAT IMPACT
MEANS TO ME

Earlier, you wrote down the answers to the following questions in your Personal Rulebook.

+ What are the three most important things you desire to have in your life?

+ Why are they important to you?

+ What is stopping you from having these things in your life?

Revisit this Play in your Personal Rulebook, and using the concepts you've just learned, let's now map out a game plan for you. You'll be guided to write down your thoughts in a few places, but also take notes on any ideas or thoughts the following steps spark.

Step 1: Clarity of Desire and Steady Determination

Start with your first "important thing" (aka your target). Think about what you want. Get really clear about it. Visualize what it looks like. Feel what it will feel like, as if you have already accomplished it. Ask yourself why you want it and think about all of the reasons you want to make it happen in your life. In the second question above, you have already listed a few reasons. Let's keep digging further to help you really make it concrete.

Write down everything you have just come up with in your mind. Start with the general idea and get more and more specific as you feel the momentum build in you as you visualize what you want. Create a determination within you that inspires you, meaning it pulls you toward your goal. When we are inspired, we are drawn to something; we don't have to push to make something happen. When you find the reasons that support *why* you want something, you find the inspiration to realize that dream.

Step 2: True Power

Start owning your power to create the life you want. Start telling yourself all the reasons you deserve to have everything you want in life. Think about the concept that you could actually, deliberately, choose to have whatever you want. For some, the thought that they deserve or can choose to have whatever they want in life is quite a stretch because of what they have been taught by others or experiences they've had. If this happens to be you, I know that this may be a very difficult step. But I promise you that if you will keep bringing the idea back to your heart, when your mind tells you, "Uh . . . I don't think so. It's never worked out that way before. You are worthless. You can't do it. You don't deserve to have unlimited joy and happiness . . ." you will begin to feel your true power. Just keep bringing it back to your heart with the intention of feeling the truth that lies within you.

Step 3: Integration

Start appreciating all of the things you do well and find reasons to be grateful for who you are. Start incorporating the things that make you unique into the different aspects of your life. Think about what you can infuse into your life that will make people say, "Oh, that is soooo you!" For example, I have been all about balance for many years. People in my life, whether they are from work or from my personal relationships, know that I love balance. I talk about it. I teach it. I live with the clarity that I want it in my life and am steadily determined to maintain it.

My financial advisory office is very *feng shui.* There are candles, plants galore, a wall fountain, a saltwater fish tank, oversized leather recliner chairs in front of an electric fireplace, a big screen television above playing a loop of beautiful nature scenes, and relaxing music in the background, just to name a few characteristics. These are not your typical financial advisor office decorations, yet when people—clients or coworkers—first come to my new office, they all say, "This is so Karri!"

Working in the financial industry, helping people plan their financial future, investing their money, and holding their hands through scary stock-market drops can be a stressful work environment. For me, it was crucial that I create a space that would support a peaceful and relaxing state. It not only works for me, but it helps my clients maintain more emotional balance, too. Countless times, I have had clients say they feel so much better after sitting in the recliners for ten minutes and watching the beautiful nature scenes while they waited for me to bring them back for our appointment.

Candles and fish tanks might not be your thing, but I'm sure you can think of five things right now that are. Think about how you can incorporate those "things" that represent who you are into your life. Then start integrating them.

Step 4: Transformation

As you start integrating these aspects and awarenesses about your true Self into your life, make time and space to allow for transformation. Take advantage of opportunities for personal growth. What training could you sign up for, or what group could you join to help you grow? Think about why something feels right to you or maybe why it feels wrong; solidify those awarenesses by writing them down. When you run into a challenge, stop to take a closer look at the situation. Ask yourself questions about it. Dig deep to see what you can learn about yourself or others involved. Transformation happens when we are open to new possibilities and we are willing to accept something new.

An important part of transformation is to recognize, enjoy, and celebrate your metamorphosis. Even if it is just for a few minutes, take time to spread your wings and fly like a butterfly. This might be sharing your achievement with a friend over a glass of wine. It might be taking time daily to be grateful for who you have now become, what you have accomplished, and the way you feel. It might even be dancing in your living room to your favorite tunes. Set your intention to have greater awareness about yourself. Self-actualization is the epitome of MASTERY transformation.

Step 5: Manifestation

Knowing that emotional manifestation is the first part of manifesting, what can you do to create that emotional energetic frequency in your body? How could you build into your days more ways to envision your outcome? Could you meditate every morning and spend time prior to that meditation envisioning your life as if you have already achieved your dream? How could you feel your desire? Could you talk about what you want in the present tense, as though you already have it, to help get those feelings into your body? Could you daydream about it and imagine yourself truly living it?

There is no right or wrong way with this one. Whatever way seems right to you is the right way or ways. The key is to *feel* the positive and abundant nature of your goal. If you have mixed emotions about what you want to manifest, you will manifest mixed outcomes.

For the physical part of the equation, think about what has already shown up that is adding to your success in reaching your target. Celebrate and be grateful for it. Set an intention to consciously look for more signs that point you in the right direction. As you begin to see physical manifestations, milk the wonderful feelings of joy, excitement, anticipation, and inspiration that it brings. Milking those feeling will build your momentum and help you realize your vision faster.

Step 6: Hitting the Bull's-Eye

Think about all of your strengths. What are you really good at? What do you enjoy most? What innate gifts were you just born with that can help you as you aim toward your target? How can you use the talents you already have to help you? How can you hone those skills to increase your performance and feel success?

If you wanted to master this area or thing in your life, what would you need to do to make that happen? This one question alone will give you tremendous insight into your game plan.

Deep down, we each have our own answers. You know, deep down, what you need to do to actualize your dream. And if you are not really sure what to do, you intuitively know who you should ask to help you figure out what to do. Part of the MASTERY game of Hide & Seek is recognizing that when you find your true Self, your *You*, you find answers that only *You* can know. Those answers help you line up your aim and hit the bull's-eye.

Practice

Wow! Did you just answer all of those questions to determine the steps toward your first target? If not, go back now and spend just two minutes on each step. Twelve minutes of your time focusing your attention is a bargain in exchange for the ability to maximize your impact in one of the most important areas of your life. The majority of people are unwilling to do this transformational work, which is the key to all success in life. Do it for yourself. Do it for all the reasons you wrote down at the beginning of this Personal Rulebook Play. Do it because it is a proven process that can give you the thing we all want at the core of our beings . . . joy.

Once you've completed the game plan for your first "thing," go through and create a game plan using this same process for each of the other two important targets you wrote down at the beginning of this Personal Rulebook Play.

When you were a kid playing Hide & Seek with your friends, you probably were a little lost the first time you got in the game. You had to learn all the rules, you didn't know all the best hiding spots, and you were trying to figure out where you fit in. But as you played the game again and again, you became more comfortable with yourself and with the overall experience of the game. As you go through the process of using these new tools to maximize your impact, you will find that as you do it over and over again, it, too, will become second nature and a natural part of your journey.

CHAPTER FIVE

ACHIEVE THROUGH ALIGNMENT

*T*he *A* in *MASTERY* stands for *Achieve through Alignment.* Alignment is everything. Alignment equals balance; balance equals alignment. Alignment with what? With your true Self. The *You* that you're seeking in your MASTERY game of Hide & Seek.

When you understand how to live in alignment with who you are at the very core of your nature, you learn how to create the life you want, rather than feeling like life is happening *to* you. There is a power that comes from understanding the basic laws that govern how we feel in any given moment, and our alignment directly impacts the feelings we have in that moment. For example, if our beliefs and our wants are not aligned, we experience inner turmoil. The formula for true happiness is to have your beliefs and values equal your reality. When your life is playing out the way you think it should, you feel happy. Negative feelings of sadness, frustration, irritation, or general unhappiness all stem from your life not being aligned with the picture in your mind of what you believe it should be.

Think about the last time you were upset or felt discord about something. It wasn't because everything was hunky dory with rainbows and butterflies, was it? I bet you will discover that the actuality of the situation didn't match what you thought it should be. For example, maybe you were frustrated with a coworker who was challenging your plan for a project you were working on together. Why were you frustrated? Most likely because your coworker's view was different from yours, and your internal "belief" is that your way was the right way. The situation was not matching up with your belief. If your belief was to always be open to every idea to see if it enhances the project, you would have likely felt more curiosity than frustration.

Another example of a common "yucky" feeling that I've personally discovered in my own life is irritation. I can always trace the irritation back to alignment. If I'm irritated with my kids, it's often because I am spending time in my head instead of being in my heart so I could offer them the attention that every child naturally craves. Once I became aware of this pattern, I was able to get clear about what my belief is around the way I interact with my kids. I want to be loving, nurturing, and kind, so I made a decision to live in alignment with that belief. I've learned to catch myself when I feel the irritation starting, and remind myself to get out of my head and into my heart. It's beautiful. Rather than feeling the contention and internal turmoil that comes from feeling irritation, I now use the irritation (yes, it still comes!) as a trigger that I am not in alignment. It allows me to be gentle with myself and not feel guilty about the negative emotion, but rather feel grateful for it, which then helps me find alignment and happier emotions.

In our world, where achievement plays such a big part in society, people can often get caught up in the achievement part of the equation and forget about the alignment part. But to become a master of achievement, there is one basic need, and that is to be aligned with your true Self. As you are playing your MASTERY games of Hide & Seek, you're searching for alignment with *You*. This alignment is the key to your success in any area of your life.

UNIVERSAL LAWS FOR ACHIEVING ALIGNMENT

How do you find alignment? That's a good question, and the answer is that it's different for each one of us. We are each exploring this life and living a different reality from anyone else on earth so there is no cookie-cutter answer that will walk you step-by-step into alignment. That's the bad news. The good news is that there are some universal truths that apply to all of us and when we understand and apply these truths, we are able to discover our own personal formula for alignment.

> *Some universal truths apply to all of us and when*
> *we understand and apply these truths, we are able to*
> *discover our own personal formula for alignment.*

I find the idea of universal truths, or "laws," as we call them in the modern world, fascinating. For example, the law of gravity. This is an indisputable law that science has proven and we see the effects and conclusive evidence of its existence every moment of our lives. We don't question the law of gravity. We know it exists even though we can't touch it or hear it or even see it. We see the effects of it and we feel its presence in our lives. It is a universal law that affects everyone and everything on earth.

There are other laws that date back over 5,000 years from ancient Egypt to ancient Greece, and from the Vedic tradition in ancient India, that all have a common thread as well. These laws, like the law of gravity, are ever present and play a significant role in your MASTERY game of Hide & Seek. These Universal Laws impact your ability to find alignment with your true Self. Their dynamic presence in your life is one that can leave you feeling confused and helpless, or enlightened and empowered.

When you understand these Universal Laws, you can use them to your advantage and achieve whatever you desire, whether that is related to work, home, relationships, personal growth, health, or financial abundance. We are all on equal playing fields when it comes to these laws. Like the law of gravity, they are unwavering, dependable, and absolute. There are no favorites on the playing field, and these laws are not like referees, who can subjectively choose what to call. These "universal referees" are always right on the money with the calls and never need to go back to look at an instant replay.

I have been thinking about what to share in this chapter, researching the known spiritual laws and coming up with how they relate to your MASTERY game, and trying to decide what is most important for you to know so that you can Achieve through Alignment. I hear Robin Williams's voice as the genie from the Disney movie *Aladdin*. He says: "Phenomenal cosmic powers . . . itty-bitty living space." Each of these laws has multiple books written about it, so how in the heck do I do them justice in one chapter?

There are eight laws that we'll touch on, and I believe they can be narrowed down to three groups to help you achieve a level of mastery in your lifelong quest for alignment. So I will attempt to condense the phenomenal cosmic powers down to that itty-bitty living space that you can hold in your hand. Well, maybe holding them in your head and heart is a better choice for this metaphor. Either way, let's take a look at how you can use these powerful laws to create a powerful life.

As you've learned, the overall elements of the MASTERY game of Hide & Seek are: 1) Knowing the Rules, 2) Understanding How to Play the Game, 3) Learning the Game, 4) Discovering Your Truth, 5) Finding Your Balance, and 6) Ready or Not, Here I Come. The Universal Laws discussed in this chapter fall within Learning the Game.

You can know the rules and understand how to play the game, but without learning the territory of the game and the dynamic energies that make up the experience of your game, it will be like playing in the pitch black with no light—without awareness of the unlimited light that is available for you to tap into. It's like you are the genie from the lamp without being aware of your powers. Once you understand that you have the ability to tap into these Universal Laws, or truths, you will supercharge your powers and have the ability to win at whatever you do.

Your MASTERY "power menu" consists of eight laws:

- The Law of Mentalism
- The Law of Correspondence
- The Law of Polarity
- The Law of Gender
- The Law of Rhythm
- The Law of Vibration
- The Law of Cause and Effect
- The Law of Attraction

I want to impress upon you the importance of the Universal Laws you are about to absorb. I also want to encourage you to keep moving through this chapter even if you find one or more of these laws difficult to grasp. We are reviewing laws that form the basis of our universe. These are deep concepts, and as you will learn from these laws, your ability to connect and understand them will depend upon your own state of being as you are studying them. Don't be discouraged if something doesn't resonate with you the first time you read it. Just keep moving through the rest of the laws and onto the other aspects of your MASTERY game of Hide & Seek. The laws you need to understand will resonate with you when the time is right, I promise. Remember, your Hide & Seek games are meant to be challenging, but most important, they are meant to be fun!

For the purpose of the MASTERY game of Hide & Seek, these laws are separated into three groups so that you can more easily grasp the concepts within a larger framework. Then you will learn how to apply them to achieve the life you desire.

THE MENTAL FOCUS
AND CONNECTEDNESS GROUP

The first group consists of the Law of Mentalism and the Law of Correspondence. The Law of Mentalism says that all is mind, that everything we see and experience originates from the mental realm, and that our individual minds are part of the Universal Mind. The Law of Mentalism tells us that our reality is manifested from the thoughts in our mind. So basically, we think it, dream it, visualize it, or imagine it before it becomes "real" in the physical world.

The Law of Correspondence tells us that everything on the physical, mental, and spiritual realms is connected. It also states that the same patterns are expressed on all levels of existence—whether that is at the electron level or a planetary level. The Law of Correspondence tells us that everything is connected and when we understand something on one level, we can, potentially, understand it at any level.

These two laws can be grouped together for our purposes of MASTERY because they both help us find alignment through their ability to connect us with our Soul, which is the *You* we are looking for in our Hide & Seek games. They help us to see that what we think and what we experience are connected. They help us to understand that when we feel emotionally drained, we will also feel physically exhausted. They give us the foundation to see that we are all connected to the bigger picture and that even the smallest things can make an impact in our lives.

The Law of Mentalism

Let's apply this to something practical in your life to help you get a better grasp of how you can master alignment. Looking at the Law of Mentalism, you will see the role of mental focus and its ability to radically impact your life experience. When you exercise your ability to focus your attention on something, you increase the probability that it will happen in your life. Think about a time when you were focused, really focused, on something in particular. It may have been as simple as "I really feel like having pizza for dinner." How often when you feel a craving for something to eat, do you end up eating it shortly thereafter? This is a very simplistic example of this law, but I want you to see that these laws affect us on every level.

You can take this further and think about a time when you wanted to achieve a goal, such as being in the relationship of your dreams. Before that person came into your life, what were you thinking about them? Did you create a list with all of the characteristics you wanted this person to have? Did you consciously open yourself up emotionally to the possibilities of finding your dream mate? Did you imagine and daydream about the things you would do together and how you would feel when you were falling madly in love?

If a relationship example is not doing it for you, then maybe it was your dream job. Was the job constantly on your mind? Did you spend time researching the company, the role, and how you would be able to create a positive impact on the business? Did you set a goal about how much you wanted to earn? Did you imagine yourself in the role and visualize how you would feel sitting at your desk or walking into the building?

These are each examples of how we are able to create something in our life by simply focusing our mental attention on what we want. Your mental focus is directly related to what you experience in your life. This has tremendous power if you choose to purposefully use it. Let me say that again: Your mental focus has tremendous power if you choose to purposefully use it. That means your thoughts really do create your reality. And choosing how you want to focus your mental attention will shape your experiences. This is not about playing Jedi mind tricks. It is simply about the fact that what we put our attention on grows stronger in our lives. The reason I say this law has tremendous power when you purposefully use it is because it is an immutable law. *Immutable* means that it is absolute and cannot be changed or transcended. The law doesn't care whether you are using it for what you *want* to create in your life or what you *don't want* to create in your life. It just is.

Your mental focus has tremendous power
if you choose to purposefully use it.

For instance, if you are mentally focused on how horrible your relationship is and you are constantly thinking about what you don't like, you will continue to be unfulfilled in your relationship. If you are constantly thinking about how you don't have any money and there is always another bill waiting for you in the mailbox, you will continue to find yourself struggling financially to make ends meet. Until you mentally focus on what you want in your life, you will continue to reap the benefits—meaning scarcity—of your thoughts.

The good news is that you can Achieve through Alignment by using the Law of Mentalism. By understanding this law and aligning your thoughts with your desires in life, you will begin to see the manifestations. You don't have to take my word for it. Just try doing it. Start thinking about what you really want in your life. Put your focus on it and watch how opportunities, inspirations, coincidences, and other ideas start showing up in your life. Try not to have rigid time expectations. They may happen immediately, or some may take a while. Either way, you will begin to see that when your thoughts and desires are aligned, you will start to purposefully create the life you want. Or . . . you may see that you are aligning your thoughts with what you don't want in your life and you will be creating the life you *don't* want. It's your choice how you want to experiment with this law. I personally recommend focusing on what you do want. It's a heck of a lot more fun!

THE LAW OF MENTALISM IN MY LIFE

Get out your Personal Rulebook. Consider how the Law of Mentalism shows up in your life, and then respond to the following:

✦ What three ways can you see the effect of your mental focus in your life?

✦ Do you see it in your relationships? How could you use it to enhance the relationships?

✦ Do you use it to your advantage in your work? If not, how could you?

✦ How does it show up in your life overall—positively or negatively? Can you see a pattern in the tone of your mental thoughts?

The Law of Correspondence

The Law of Mentalism ties into the Law of Correspondence because you can use them in similar ways by seeing how they prove our connectedness with all that is. Just as you can use your mental connection to create manifestations, you can also use the fact that everything is connected to design the masterpiece you call your life. When you get the fact that everything is connected, even in the smallest ways, you will begin to realize that what you do, what you say, how you feel, and what you think influence your experience.

Let's make that statement a little more tangible. Have you ever been physically tired or started getting sick, and then realized that your thoughts started to become more negative? I use this example because I have personally experienced it. I tend to be a very positive person by nature, but when I am physically off balance because I am really tired, mentally exhausted, or starting to get sick, I can noticeably see my thoughts turn more negative, and my perspective become more uncertain. This is an example of the Law of Correspondence. The big C Law is constantly showing us that the physical, mental, and spiritual realms are connected. You begin to have more negative emotions or thoughts because your physical being is operating at a lower energetic frequency. From the spiritual perspective, you have closed yourself off—to some extent—from the always loving, accepting, and positive Soul that is *You*. Your Spirit will not be negative or uncertain; that is one thing that you can always count on.

Have you ever heard stories about the phenomenon of twins who experience the same emotions or have an intuition that something is wrong with the other, even when they are on opposite ends of the country? How about the fact that birds know when and where to migrate? Or that a flock of birds will fly in sync and turn, as a group, in a split second? These are examples of ways that we are connected, in both physical and nonphysical ways. Some of these ways we haven't been able to even consciously comprehend.

I recently watched a video on YouTube of an experiment attempting to prove that when we "mirror" another person, we can actually tap into their energetic field and feel the same emotions or see visions in our mind of what they are thinking about. In the video, two men were asked to stand about five feet apart. Man number one was asked to imagine an experience he had been through where he saved a boy who had fallen on the tracks of the city subway. While the train was quickly approaching, he jumped onto the tracks, grabbed the boy, and saved his life with only seconds to spare. It was obviously a very intense and emotional experience. He was asked to imagine the experience and, without speaking, feel the emotions as he relived the experience in his mind.

The second man was asked to simply look at man number one and mirror, or mimic, his every movement, be it as subtle as facial expressions or posture. As he mirrored the first man for a few minutes, he began to connect with his energy field. He started to feel emotions of fear, intensity, and the same emotions the first man was feeling as he relived his experience. The second man even reported having the image of a subway train flash in his mind prior to learning anything about man number one.

This is one of many examples of the power of mirroring. Mirroring has been used for years to help people in business. It has been taught as a way to gain rapport with someone. It allows a prospect, client, or teammate to feel that you understand him or her and empathize with his or her feelings. Even when someone has no idea you are using a mirror technique (kind of the whole point!), they will feel a connection with you and have no conscious idea why.

Mirroring is just one example of how we have been able to measure the Law of Correspondence. We are all connected, and when we are able to align with and use that ability to connect, we can use it to our advantage.

Remember when the tsunami hit Thailand in 2004? The news reported that people saw animals running to higher ground prior to the tsunami hitting. How did the animals know that danger was approaching? Because animals spend the majority of their time in alignment—alignment with their surroundings, alignment by not having mental thoughts holding them back, and alignment with the present moment. Animals are wonderful teachers of the Law of Correspondence and connectedness. Just as we discussed knowing when to be still and when to move in your games of Hide & Seek, being in tune with your connectedness to God will help you know when to move and when to stay in life situations.

For example, let's say you are in a business meeting. By staying connected, you are able to see how the other people in the room are feeling about what is being discussed. By staying connected you are able to "read between the lines" and have a sense of how your message or product is being received. By staying connected you are able to navigate the conversation and look for ways to draw out the best in your team and create a win-win situation for everyone involved. You might even be so connected that you notice people haven't been drinking water and they are starting to get dehydrated. By offering everyone a drink, you can revive their physical energy, which in turn will increase their mental clarity and make the meeting more productive.

The Law of Correspondence tells us that everything originates from one Source. The evidence is indisputable that we are all connected. When we align with that connectedness, we are able to master any area of our lives. This is one way you Achieve through Alignment. You connect with all that you are, and you achieve your goals and desires by lining up who you are with what you want. If you recognize that everything in your life is teaching you something on some level and that what you learn is connected to other things in your life, you can use this newfound awareness to create your idea of success.

What I have found most interesting in my own life is the fact that the depth to the connectedness is infinite. Just when I think I have mastered a level of understanding of this Law of Correspondence, another "aha" moment will happen for me and I will become aware of a new level of connectedness. Something new will come into my life that will teach me how I am connected to something that I'd never imagined before and it will blow my mind.

An example is Dr. Masaru Emoto's incredible work with water crystals. This brilliant pioneer studied the ability of human consciousness to influence the way water crystalizes. Among a series of experiments, Dr. Emoto taped words like *love, grace,* and *happiness* to a petri dish of water. The water was then frozen, and the ice crystals were viewed under a microscope. The frozen water revealed beautiful crystals with symmetrical designs. When he repeated the process with words like *hate, destroy, and revenge,* the crystals that formed were broken, asymmetrical, and deformed. The water responded to the intention of the words that were simply taped onto the petri dish! Learning of Emoto's work was one of those mind-blowing moments for me that deepened my awareness of how everything in our world ties together—from our thoughts to our emotions to tangible elements such as water.

I recently watched a YouTube video showing another experiment by Dr. Emoto. In this one, he put water and rice into three glass beakers. For the next thirty days he said, "Thank you" to the first glass. He said, "You're an idiot" to the second glass, and he completely ignored the third glass. After thirty days, the rice in the first beaker had fermented and was giving off a pleasant aroma. The rice in the second beaker had turned black. And the rice in the third beaker had begun to rot. It was a remarkable visual of how we are connected to everything. If this is the response when you ignore or degrade water and rice, can you imagine how those same intentions and behaviors impact children, plants, or animals?

It is plain and simple, yet profoundly complex. We all come from one Source. We all come from God. Therefore, we are all connected on different levels and to infinite depths. The MASTERY message in all of this is to know you are not alone. While you may feel that you are a single individual and may sometimes feel like you are all alone in this world, know that it is absolutely an illusion of your mind. You are infinitely connected to everyone and everything around you. Remember as a kid, how fun it was to play Hide & Seek with your friends at twilight? That fun came through your connection to everyone playing together. You were aligned with the Law of Correspondence and you felt the wholeness—and joy—that comes when that happens.

You are infinitely connected to everyone
and everything around you.

Personal Rulebook Play
MY CONNECTIONS

Get your Personal Rulebook out and write down at least two ways that you can recognize your connection to other people, places, or things. Then, respond to the following:

+ Do you recognize the connection because of a feeling?

+ Can you visually see how your connection impacts you or someone else, such as the observations with the rice experiment? Or possibly how your children respond to your mood?

+ How could you proactively add this law to your awareness and begin using it to help you achieve your goals and dreams for your life?

+ Are there ways that you can combine your knowledge of mental focus and connectedness to improve your relationships? Your professional career? Your personal feelings of connectedness with the world around you?

THE OPPOSITES AND FLOW GROUP

The next group is made up of three laws: the Law of Polarity, the Law of Gender, and the Law of Rhythm . These three laws are *mutable* laws, meaning that when we have mastered them, we have the ability to transcend or learn how to use them in better ways to create a more positive experience. I grouped these three Universal Laws together because they represent the dynamic flow and the appearance of opposition, or duality, in our world. They also represent our need for balance. My perspective on life has been defined by balance for many years. About thirteen years ago, I began to recognize my need for balance in my own life. This is not just the coined "work-life balance" phrase that society has overused, but a balance that—like the depth of our connection—is infinite. Our desire for balance stems from these three laws. They also influence our ability to play our MASTERY games of Hide & Seek.

The Law of Polarity

Have you ever heard someone say opposites attract? I hear it used most often in reference to relationships. You can create a visual image of the Law of Polarity by thinking of a pair of magnets. A magnet has two ends or poles, a north pole and a south pole. When you take two magnets and put them together with the opposite poles facing each other, they will instantly be drawn together. Yet, when you flip one over, and put them together again with the same two poles facing each other, it is as though there is a barrier between them and they repel one another.

Everything actually has two poles and is dual in nature. Everything has an opposite, and opposites are identical in nature but different in degree. What does that mean in real-life terms? It means things that may appear to be completely opposite are really just extremes of the same thing. An example is love and hate. These are opposite ends of the spectrum of emotions. Activity and stillness are opposite forms of movement. Black and white are opposite ends of the color spectrum. There is always a binding factor that connects two opposites, which is what makes them identical in nature, but different in degree on the spectrum.

Let's now take this understanding of the Law of Polarity and make it real in your world. Where you choose to "live" on the spectrum of any given pole has an effect on your perspective and ultimately on how you experience your life. Whether you see something as good or bad, whether you feel supported or cheated, whether you have a positive or negative outlook—they all boil down to your perspective about something.

When you understand that your experience is shaped by your perspective of what is happening, you are able to choose the experience you have by consciously choosing the perspective you see it from. There are people who have had the same parents, gone to the same school, and lived in the same home throughout their childhoods. Yet, one loved childhood and the other hated it. Each one's perspective and choice of where to live on each "pole" completely influenced the meaning of personal experiences, which in turn influenced the actual events of childhood. While they had the same tangible framework, such as parents, school, and home, they had very different experiences (actual childhood events) because of each one's personal perspective.

When we understand the Laws of the Universe, we have control over the events of our lives. This control may sometimes feel limited. You may be reading this and saying something like, "So, Karri, you are telling me that I had control over my mom's death?" No, I'm not saying you have control over everything that happens in your life. But I am saying that you have complete control over how you take in what happens in your life. The meaning and your perspective about what is happening are completely in your control. You can choose to have the perspective that your mom is gone and you are going to feel sad and lonely for years to come, or you can choose to celebrate her life and continue to connect with her spirit, which remains intensely focused on you for the rest of your life.

The Law of Polarity helps us understand how the role of opposites plays out in our lives. You can Achieve through Alignment by choosing where you want to align your attention and energy with the poles. You can choose if you want to align yourself with the opposite or same pole of the magnet in any given situation. Depending on your outcome, you may choose to align with the side that repels rather than the one that attracts. Every situation in your life is an opportunity to find the place on the spectrum where you feel most balanced.

Personal Rulebook Play
MASTERING THE LAW OF POLARITY

Get out your Personal Rulebook, and use this Play to start thinking about how you can begin to master the Law of Polarity in your life. Write down your answers to the following questions:

✦ Do you ever feel like there are people with whom you react like magnets with the same facing poles and it seems like you are repelling each other?

✦ If this relationship is important to you and one that you want to keep in your life, how do you think you can use this awareness of the Law of Polarity to help you have more compassion for your differences and give you insights about how to adjust your position on the magnetic pull?

✦ How could you focus on the "good" or positive pole of a situation or circumstance, even when it appears to be "bad"? Can you look for the silver lining of a situation that is currently getting you down?

✦ Can you see how your perspective impacts your experience? Is it a positive or negative impact? What could you do to align with a view that will create a more positive perspective?

The Law of Gender

This second Universal Law in this group, the Law of Gender, tells us that everything has masculine and feminine elements—from humans, plants, and animals to electrons and magnetic poles. These elements show up in the feminine as magnetic and receptive abilities, the outward expressions being love, patience, and intuition. The feminine has a gentle and quiet, yet profoundly powerful, nature to it. The power of the feminine nature has the ability to literally draw you in.

The masculine shows up as dynamic and initiatory abilities. The outward expressions of the masculine are logic, dynamic energy, and self-reliance. These elements have an intense and forceful power. They make things happen. They get stuff done. They are big and swift.

Everything and everyone has both the masculine and feminine qualities to some degree. In fact, it is essential that we have both for us to be whole. We will go into more detail about how to combine, balance, and step into your masculine and feminine energies in Chapter 7: Think with Compassion. For now, it's necessary to understand how the Law of Gender affects your life and how your ability to align with it will help you achieve your goals.

The basic principle to remember so that you can make this law practical in your world is:

Masculine = Dynamic   **Feminine = Magnetic**

Your masculine energy helps you to achieve by:

- ✦ Utilizing your dynamic energy
- ✦ Knowing your limits and boundaries
- ✦ Being flexible and open to opportunities that can expand your leadership

Each of these elements expresses the dynamic qualities that the masculine gives you when you align with it. When you feel inspired to take action, you are using your masculine energy to initiate your movement. For instance, you want to get stuff done around the house. Whether it is doing laundry or working on a project in the garage, you are using your masculine energy when you start telling yourself you need to get it done.

When you understand your limits and boundaries, you are tapping into your masculine energy to help you get your bearings so that you can determine where and how to move. For example, if you were in charge of a project—at work or at home—you might begin by figuring out what your outcome will be, how you want to approach it, and what you are willing or not willing to do. Using these masculine qualities helps you logically organize the project so you can move into it with a plan.

When you want to expand your ability to lead, you are also using your masculine qualities to be flexible and open to the opportunities that will help you. While there are outstanding men and women leaders in our world, their ability to become an effective leader is driven by their masculine qualities. As a quick side note, don't let this idea fool you into thinking that the feminine energy is not important in this example. These leaders would not be outstanding if they were not able to use both their masculine *and* feminine energies. The masculine energy, though, is what helps them look for the opportunity for growth and drives them to continue moving toward their goal. Whether you want to be the leader of others, or simply be an outstanding leader of yourself, this masculine energy will help you accomplish this goal.

Personal Rulebook Play
MY MASCULINE ENERGY

Get out your Personal Rulebook, and think about how masculine energy shows up in your life. Jot down some personal examples of how you use it and answer the following questions:

✦ Can you recognize the dynamic, outward moving, strong, dominant, logical, intellectual, and self-reliant nature of this masculine energy?

✦ How do you use this force in your life? Do you use it in a positive or negative way?

✦ Does your masculine energy dominate your life? Do you let it drive you to a point where it can actually become detrimental to achieving your goals because it has become too dominant?

✦ What are some ways that you use your masculine energy to your advantage? How does it help you in your success at work or at home?

For you to make progress toward your goals in life, you will need to connect with the dynamic masculine energy within you. And at the same time, you will also need to connect with your feminine energy. I know, if you are a big, strong man, you might be thinking about skipping this section, but WAIT . . . I'm not going to ask you to "act like a girl." I'm just going to help you see how the Law of Gender will show you the feminine qualities that will help you reach the outcomes you want in life. Keep in mind that it's still important to recognize that there are many "girls" out there who can kick some serious ass when they want to. That is their masculine energy shining through. Feminine energy is a softer, yet still very powerful, energy that I want to help you connect with right now.

Once again, the basic principle to make this law practical in your world is:

Masculine = Dynamic   Feminine = Magnetic

Your feminine energy helps you to achieve by:

✦ Using your communication and leadership skills

✦ Guiding you to follow what has heart and meaning

✦ Trusting your own truth and authenticity

Each of these elements expresses the magnetic qualities the feminine gives you when you align with it. When you connect with a group of team members who have varying personalities through effective communication, you are using your feminine energy to lead. Without this ability, you would not be an effective leader. A person in power who dominates relationships with one-sided communication is a dictator, and people do not willingly follow a dictator. On the other hand, a leader who is able to make people feel heard while sharing his or her own vision will elicit the very best from the team.

When you follow what has heart and meaning to you, you tap into your feminine energy by listening to your inner wisdom. The feminine wisdom is a quiet, yet very powerful knowing within each of us that allows us to listen to the deepest desires of our Soul. Can you remember a time when you were inspired to do something in your life? It may have been creating a family so you could share your life with others you deeply love. It may have been the yearning to give back by participating in a local charity or organization whose purpose aligned with your beliefs. It may have even been a project at work you felt so passionate about that you couldn't stop thinking about it or working on it, even after you left the office. Whatever area of your life it may be in, following what has heart and meaning to you is part of how your feminine energy shows up in your life.

The final way you can achieve by using your feminine energy is by trusting your own truth and authenticity. This one is actually very simple, yet it can be the most difficult for many people. Your truth and authenticity is what your MASTERY games of Hide & Seek are all about. Discovering what feels best to you, what feels right to you in any given situation, and knowing the path that you feel, intuitively —not always logically—makes the most sense. Sometimes the ability to just be real can seem counterintuitive, especially in a society where individuals and companies want others to accept them. Wanting to influence others by trying to put your best foot forward can sometimes lead you away from your truth and authenticity rather than toward it.

This reminds me of a part in the movie, *What to Expect When You're Expecting*. Elizabeth Banks's character, Wendy, has a breastfeeding boutique called The Breast Choice, and she is also extremely pregnant. She is scheduled to speak at a baby-themed convention. While the speech she has prepared is all about the joys and wonder of pregnancy, she is personally having a horrible pregnancy experience. When she gets up in front of the group, she breaks down and bursts out into a speech about how much the process sucks. Someone in the audience films the outburst and it goes viral on YouTube. The next day, when she sees the video, she is horrified. Yet, when she arrives at her boutique, it is flooded with customers who saw her and were drawn to her store and to Wendy.

Why were people flocking to Wendy's store? Because they related to the authenticity and realness of her outburst. They loved that she was willing to speak her truth. It was refreshing, and they were drawn to it. This is a great example of the magnetic quality of the feminine energy. Oftentimes, we think we need to control how we will attract customers to our business or people in our lives. In reality, it is when we step into the truth of who we are that others feel drawn to us. This example reminds us that we don't have to try so hard. We just have to be ourselves and allow the magnetic qualities of who we are to bring the right people into our lives.

Personal Rulebook Play
MY FEMININE ENERGY

Grab your Personal Rulebook and think about how the feminine energy shows up in your life. Then, respond to the following questions:

- Can you recognize the magnetic, inward moving, gentle, receptive, patient, and loving feminine energy?

- How do you use this soft, yet profoundly powerful, quality in your life? Do you see it in a positive or negative way?

- Do you allow yourself to connect to your feminine energy? Can you see how using the qualities of the feminine energy can help you to achieve your goals?

When you align with the Law of Gender, you are honoring the different ways things show up in you and in the world. Without each of the properties of the masculine and the feminine, the dynamics of our world would be lopsided and, quite frankly, pretty boring. The differences between the masculine and the feminine create variety, attraction, and dynamic interplay. As you play with the balance of these two forces, have fun with how they interact and move you in different directions to help you achieve your goals. Success and abundance are the results of being dynamically assertive (masculine) and being magnetically open (feminine). Connect with these two energies, get inspired, and be playful as you explore these aspects of yourself!

The Law of Rhythm

The last Universal Law in this group is the Law of Rhythm. This law tells us that everything flows in and out. There is a rise and fall, just like a tide. There is a pendulum swing, as everything cycles from one side to another. This law states that when anything reaches a point of culmination, the backward swing begins, almost unnoticeably, until a time comes when the movement has been totally reversed. Then, the forward movement begins again, and the process repeats itself.

This law is easy for us to see in the rise and fall of the ocean waves, the phases of the moon, the shifting from positive to negative thoughts, cycles of success and failure, and even the rise and fall of great empires. It happens in games all the time as momentum shifts from one team to another. Didn't you have times as a kid when almost everyone on your team was caught, waiting at home base, and just then . . . the last remaining teammate sneaks up and frees everyone? All of a sudden the game is no longer almost over, and your team's rhythm is stacked on your side of the pendulum.

The Law of Rhythm explains the flow of everything in life. We experience this flow all the time. It happens in the biggest and smallest of ways. This flow is constantly happening in our bodies at a cellular level, as they are constantly adjusting to the changing environment we create through the process of living our lives. Our emotions can shift from depression to anger to stress to joy to the next emotion on the list. As we go through these shifts, the Law of Rhythm expresses itself once again.

By aligning with the principles of this law to help us achieve in our lives, we are able to use the natural rhythm and flow of all that is to guide our lives in the direction we desire. If we are on a path that is at odds with our goals and dreams, it hurts our ability to achieve those goals and dreams. But when we are able to shift the momentum of the pendulum in a direction that is in alignment with our goals and dreams, we are able to create a life filled with what we want.

For example, let's say you're having a bad day. You are feeling negative and discouraged about something that is going on, and the thoughts in your mind are *Life sucks* or *I'm always running into roadblocks*. If you want to shift your thoughts from negative to positive, you could use the idea of the pendulum to make the shift. You may start by telling yourself, *This, too, shall pass.* (This is a statement that actually holds true for anything in life.) You may then say, *This isn't the worse day of my life. I have many things to be thankful for.* Or *This is a bummer, but it is only a setback, and I have too much going for me to let this get me down.* What these thoughts begin to do is slow down the momentum of the pendulum in the negative direction.

Once you can get it to slow down, you can begin to start the "unnoticeable" shift back in the other direction. You might start to think, *This could actually be an opportunity for me to learn something that will help me as I move forward.* You might then say, *How could I use this to improve who I am and how I show up in my life?* This could then start you on a more positive trajectory, leading you to feelings of *I got this*, or *I can do this* rather than thoughts that don't support your life in a positive way.

You may also see this concept of flow show up in how you

approach your health. If you struggle with weight or other health issues, you can use the Law of Rhythm to help you in your quest for strength, vitality, and radiance. It begins again by slowing the momentum of the direction you are currently headed. Your first objective is to accept where you are, which is a crucial step to applying this process, because acceptance helps you align with what you want rather than continuing to resist what it is you are fighting against. Remember the principle of focus, which we talked about in Rule #2: Designate the Boundaries for your MASTERY games of Hide & Seek? Your ability to focus, and what you choose to focus on, has tremendous influence over what unfolds in your life. What you focus on grows stronger. When you continue to push against something, such as feeling frustrated or ashamed that you are overweight, for example, you just make it more difficult to shift the momentum of the pendulum in the other direction. By accepting who you are right now, in this moment, you give yourself the space to become who you want to be and allow for the pendulum to swing in the other direction. So . . . you accept where you are, and then you begin to use the idea of balance and flow to move yourself in a healthier direction.

By accepting who you are right now, in this moment, you give yourself the space to become who you want to be.

You could start by thinking about one thing you could do each day for just ten minutes to help you move toward a healthier lifestyle. It could be something as simple as going for a walk or maybe stretching to begin moving your body. Give yourself a time, a place, and a commitment that you will do this for yourself to help you begin to shift your momentum. Then, once you feel the goodness that comes from this simple thing you can easily do—because if it is difficult or you don't enjoy it, you won't continue doing it—that feeling of goodness will prompt you to think about other things you can do that are also easy and enjoyable to help you live a healthier lifestyle.

I've personally been through this health example for many years and in many varieties. I can assure you that the only way to successfully navigate the shift to a healthier lifestyle is to make it enjoyable, make it simple, and *don't* make yourself feel restricted. As soon as you think it is going to be hard or that you have to limit what you enjoy or that there are twenty-five million things you have to remember to make it happen, you will stop making an effort to slow down your momentum and end up just hanging on to the pendulum for a quicker ride to the unhealthy side.

The people who have achieved most in our world are the people who are able to effectively use the Law of Rhythm to minimize the swing of the pendulum on the side that does not serve them or others in their situation. They are able to slow the momentum of the flow in one direction and allow it to shift their trajectory toward a new outcome.

Personal Rulebook Play
THE LAW OF RHYTHM AT PLAY IN MY LIFE

Get out your Personal Rulebook. Think about how the Law of Rhythm shows up in your life and answer the following questions:

+ What three ways has this law negatively impacted your achievements in the past?

+ What are two or three ways you can consciously use the principles of this law to positively influence your ability to achieve your goals in your personal life?

+ What are two or three ways you can consciously use the principles of this law in your professional life?

THE VIBRATION AND THOUGHT POWER GROUP

The final group is made up of three laws: the Law of Vibration, the Law of Cause and Effect, and the Law of Attraction. These three laws give us a practical understanding of why things happen in our lives the way they do. Have you ever wondered why something was happening to you? Why you were going through an experience that seemed unfair, or you walked in a room and could "cut the tension with a knife"? These feelings can be explained by understanding this group of laws. These laws can also help you win your MASTERY games of Hide & Seek by helping you discover the vibrational core that is really *You*. This is where you will find the answers to all of your wants and desires. And as you learn to master alignment through the principles of these laws, you will be empowered to find the vibrational *You*, which will give you a sense of inner calm and knowing that you can achieve anything you want in life.

The Law of Vibration

The Law of Vibration states that the whole Universe is a vibration. Everything moves, nothing rests, and everything is vibrating at different speeds. Science has confirmed that we are pure energy vibrating at different frequencies. Everything that we experience in the physical, mental, emotional, and spiritual realms are brought about through vibrations. Our thoughts, our feelings, and our fives senses are all vibrations.

This laws helps us to visibly measure what we talked about in the Law of Correspondence when we learned that we are all connected. We are connected through vibration, and how we vibrate has a huge impact on what we achieve. Have you ever heard the axiom "Like energy attracts like energy"? This explains how things can snowball in our lives. Have you ever had a day, week, or year where it felt like it was just one thing after another? It may have been positive or negative, but the same type of momentum seemed to be a theme of what you were experiencing. This pattern showed up because you were living in a particular vibrational frequency and were attracting similar vibrational frequencies to you.

The Law of Vibration tells us that everything is vibration. That means people, situations, and even thoughts find their way into your life in a vibrational manner. This may be a new concept to you, and if so, you may be wondering, *How am I supposed to measure my vibration without carrying around a scientific instrument all day?* Within your MASTERY games, this is an easy one to answer because you've been doing it all your life. It's second nature to you. The answer is: your emotions. Your emotions are actually your best indication of your current vibrational frequency. They are also your best instruments for leading you out of a vibrational "stuck point."

For example, if you find yourself in a situation where you just can't seem to get a break, start by looking at your own vibrational set point. If you are operating at a vibrational frequency that is in alignment with frustration, disappointment, or uncertainty, you will draw to you other circumstances or people who are vibrating—or operating—at those same frequencies. It becomes a spiral effect that continues to build momentum unless you proactively, and consciously, choose to change your vibrational stance. Consciously choosing your vibration is the key to that statement. Why? Because without being purposeful in your choice of frequency, you will end up matching whichever frequency happens to come into your vicinity (aka your life).

In this example, you can't get a break and everything seems to be going wrong for you. Good things may happen occasionally and you will briefly feel good and raise your vibration, but as soon as something negative happens and you reactively drop your vibration, you will continue to draw more of the lower-frequency people and situations to you. This is a sloppy way to focus and leads to a roller-coaster ride of emotions and experiences. As we have already learned, to become a master, you have to learn to be intentional with your focus and attention.

Thankfully, this doesn't have to be a difficult process to change the spiral you may feel trapped within. It can actually be as simple as changing your habit of whatever vibration you are offering. We have the ability to change our perspective and therefore our vibrational frequency in an instant. But, oftentimes, we develop the habit of offering a particular vibration and just keep doing it over and over again, day after day.

You can begin to change the momentum of circumstances in your life by developing habits with new frequencies. So, in our example above, you can begin to shift the momentum and bring a more positive perspective by saying to yourself, "Things do work out for me sometimes. And I know that if I begin to focus my attention on what I want, I will be able to create a life where I am able to achieve whatever I desire." This will begin to slow the negative momentum.

Once that negative momentum is slowed, you can then start to work your way toward a higher vibrational frequency, as you did using the pendulum process in the Law of Rhythm. Use that natural flow to help you cycle to a higher vibration. Higher vibrations show up in emotions such as compassion, exuberance, and love, which is the highest and subtlest of vibrations. Emotions on the opposite end of the scale show up as anger, rage, and hate, which is the densest and most base.

The vibrational set points at which you choose to live your life are affected by your thoughts. Results come to you based on these set points, and the more vibrational clarity you offer through your thoughts, and therefore, your energy, the better results you will achieve. There is an energy that is *You*. This energy feels like clarity, insight, inspiration, and knowing. This energy is what you want to seek and align with during your MASTERY games. This energy is the basis of all that you are.

Personal Rulebook Play
AT WHAT FREQUENCY AM I VIBRATING?

This Play can help you become more aware of the vibration you are offering and to purposefully choose the frequencies you want to operate from in your life. So, get out your Personal Rulebook, and for the next seven days, from the moment you wake up, begin to take note of the way you are feeling and the vibrational frequency you are offering. As you go through your day, jot down the correlations you discover between the following:

✦ The thoughts you are thinking

✦ The things you are talking about

✦ The way you are feeling

✦ The things that show up in your life

Be as objective as you can be so you can learn to start making deliberate choices about how you want to show up and offer your vibration in the world. While you may not have scientific instruments to measure and record the exact frequency of your physical energy, you can become keenly aware of how your life is unfolding by understanding your alignment with the Law of Vibration.

A very important note about the Law of Vibration: There can be a vast difference between what you verbally say and the vibrational frequency you are actually exuding. Oftentimes, we can be saying one thing, but everything else within us is vibrating at the exact opposite. Have you ever been upset and been asked, "What's wrong?" only to reply, "Nothing." This is a perfect example of feeling one way and verbally expressing something else. The Law of Vibration shows us that Universal energy doesn't care what you say; it's always responding to the vibration you are offering.

The Law of Cause and Effect

Through the Law of Vibration, we can see how the power of our thoughts creates our vibrational point of attraction. The second law in this group, the Law of Cause and Effect, tells us that every cause has an effect, and every effect has a cause. What we see in our physical, or outer world, originates from our mental, or inner world. It states that every thought, word, or action activates a specific effect that in time will manifest in your experience.

Through this law, we are able to own our life experience. The Law of Cause and Effect empowers each of us to take ownership of what happens in our lives. It states that nothing that happens or manifests in our lives is by chance or luck.

You may be thinking, *Yeah, that's nice, Karri, but there is no way a baby would choose to be born into an abusive family.* I agree that a baby would not sit down and think, *I'd like to be abused.* But I do believe that when we are born into the world, we are pure God-like energy, and we've come to explore everything that this world has to offer. I believe that from our pure spiritual perspective, we don't necessarily see things as good or bad, right or wrong, or positive and negative. Every experience is part of this life. When we come into the world, we come to participate in it, whatever it brings. It has also been my observation that many of the people who have been through the "worst" of times have gained the greatest perspective about what they want in the world, and they are then able to teach the rest of us how to live a life of more compassion, love, and joy.

Look at someone like Nelson Mandela, who had been convicted and sentenced to life in prison for his anti-apartheid activism role in South Africa. In spite of his circumstances, by directing his thoughts, he led himself to a place of compassion and love and, in doing so, changed the world. Mandela used the power of his thought to create a vision for what he wanted to experience in the world. He used the principles of the Law of Cause and Effect by creating this vision, first, in his inner world. He spent years imagining what could be and prepared himself for what he envisioned. When the time came for the vision to manifest in the physical world, he was ready to embrace it with all that he was. The effects of this one man's thought power—or inner world—in alignment with the Universal Laws created astounding results in the outer world.

Because this law applies to the spiritual, mental, and physical planes of existence, when we align with the Law of Cause and Effect, we step into our own power, the power that resides deep within each of us at the level of our Spirit. When we find our true Self, as in our MASTERY games of Hide & Seek, we connect to this infinite power and have the ability to achieve whatever we want.

It begins with our thoughts and desires. One difference between the planes of existence is that our physical world exists within a framework of time and space. Time and space, which are not present on the spiritual plane, can slow down the process of manifesting our thoughts into tangible results. Nelson Mandela was in prison for twenty-seven years! Although, if we take a little closer look at the time during which he was imprisoned, there were many things beginning to manifest as the momentum surrounding his situation built, and millions of people began to align with the energy of the situation.

Whether we are talking about Mandela or looking at your ability to envision an abundant future for yourself, can you see how everything is connected? How these Universal Laws show up everywhere and in everything? How the infinite components begin to align when your thought power is unyielding and full of clarity? This is the essence of the Law of Cause and Effect. When you visualize something in your mind (the mental plane), it is automatically created where there is no concept of time (on the spiritual plane), and you then have the ability through your perseverance, through practice, and through continued concentrated thought to manifest your desires in your life (the physical plane).

Personal Rulebook Play
WHAT DO I WANT TO CREATE?

The Law of Cause and Effect is all about creative visualization. So grab your Personal Rulebook and think about what you would like to create in your own life. It may be a relationship, a job, a vacation, a new home, or . . . anything! Be creative. You'll be guided to take some notes, but be sure to jot down any key thoughts and ideas as you do the following activities.

1. Use your thought power to create a clear vision of what you want in your mind. This first part of the process is strictly done on the mental plane. Just sit and daydream about what you want. Visualize it in your mind in the greatest detail possible. Don't allow thoughts of limitation to cloud your visualization. When you visualize, there are no boundaries and no limits. If you can imagine it, then it belongs in your vision. No questions asked.

2. Begin to lock in your vision and create as much clarity around it as possible by doing one or more of the following:

   + Write down the details of your vision.

   + Create a storyboard by drawing or pasting photos of what you want on a Poster (or even on a few journal pages in your Personal Rulebook).

   + Hang up pictures or notes where you will see them as reminders.

   + Spend time every day thinking about, and talking about, your vision.

3. Use your knowledge of alignment to line yourself up with your vision. The more you align all that you are—your thoughts, words, and actions—with your vision, the faster it will become a reality in your life.

4. As you begin to see components of your vision unfold, celebrate them! Ride the wave of joy that you feel as you achieve the next step—or success—along the way. Remember, this is your odyssey. It is meant to be an eventful and adventurous journey.

The Law of Attraction

The final law in this group is the Law of Attraction; it will sound familiar to you because we've been discussing its effects all throughout this chapter. The Law of Attraction actually is a thread that runs through all of the other laws. It is the basis of "like energy attracting like energy." It is also the reason for cause and effect. This constant, never-wavering law will always be present in your life.

For example, when you are thinking and talking about what you want, you are practicing the Law of Vibration. As you practice the vibration of what you want to attract, you are coming into alignment with that particular vibration. As you then become more and more aligned with that vibration, the Law of Attraction will bring to you inspiration (in the form of ideas) or situations that will allow your wants and desires to manifest.

This is a big one! I want to help you really grasp the concept here so you can use it in a practical way. It can be quite difficult to release our perspective on what we believe is the "reality" of our lives—our dramas and stories—and begin to focus our thoughts, our words, and our energy on what we want as we move forward. Have you ever been in a situation where you wanted something so badly, but you just couldn't stop beating the drum of what you already had?

Let's say you really want to have more money. You want to be able to use it to buy things you like, experience great restaurants, travel the world, give to charities, buy gifts for family and friends, have the freedom to do what you love, and so on. These are fantastic reasons to want more money! Yet, most people who want more money spend their time thinking about why they *don't* have more money. The Law of Attraction does not care that you are *saying* you want to have more money. It only responds to the vibration you are offering and gives you more of what matches it.

Rather than doing what most people do by spending your time talking about, thinking about, and worrying about not having enough money, you can use this law to your advantage. Most people go through their day with feelings of lack or worry surrounding the issue of money. They think about why they can't afford something. They worry about not having enough to pay the bills. They vibrationally offer the world feelings of fear, lack, and resistance.

Instead of offering up these vibrations, you could start thinking about what it would feel like if you had enough money to do everything you wanted. You could stop yourself whenever you caught yourself worrying about not having enough money. You could start appreciating and thinking about what you do have and what *is* abundant in your life. As you begin to think about the abundance you do have in your life, which might be love, energy, nature, or laughter, you will begin to practice a vibration that is more consistent with the abundance of everything . . . including money.

Spend time focusing on all those fantastic reasons mentioned above for why you might want to have more. These are the thoughts that will help you practice a vibration that will draw these experiences—and the funds needed to manifest them—to you. Start living your life with the feeling that you *do* have the money you want. Practice the vibration of abundance, even if that abundance isn't always attached to money. Once you align yourself with the vibrational frequency of abundance, the Law of Attraction will handle the rest.

Once you align yourself with the vibrational frequency of abundance, the Law of Attraction will handle the rest.

A quick note here: Keep in mind that there is a difference between *spending* money and *feeling* what it is like to have the money you want. I'm not suggesting you start using credit cards to buy stuff you can't afford. I'm suggesting you practice *the feeling* having money would give you. Getting into debt would only create more feelings of fear and lack, which would cause you to offer a vibration of . . . you guessed it—lack.

Personal Rulebook Play
THE LAW OF ATTRACTION
AT PLAY IN MY LIFE

Grab your Personal Rulebook, and start thinking about an area of your life where the Law of Attraction is bringing you more of what you *don't* want. Think about how you might begin practicing a vibrational frequency at the other end of the pendulum's path. Then come up with a couple of responses for each of the following questions:

◆ What, specifically, could you start thinking in order to slow your current momentum that would be a step in the right vibrational direction?

◆ What, specifically, could you say or start talking about that would help you practice a new vibration?

◆ What, specifically, could you eliminate from your life that would help you to begin focusing on what you want rather than staying stuck in your current story or situation?

When you learn how to use the Law of Attraction in alignment with all of the other Universal Laws discussed in this chapter, your ability to achieve is truly unlimited. This law brings together infinite components to create the experience called life.

Your goal now is to personally apply these concepts in your MASTERY games of Hide & Seek. When you understand these laws intellectually and are able to implement that understanding into your life, you are then able to find *You*. Once you find *You*, it is then possible to Maximize Your Impact and Achieve through Alignment at will. You are no longer searching aimlessly in the dark wondering how to play the game. You get it! You get that you have the power within you. So congratulations! Through this new understanding, you have taken the first steps toward becoming a master of your own life.

Every master has learned how to align with his or her true Self, the *You* within. Masters are considered masters of something because they have aligned with the inspiration within them, and they are allowing it to flow through them in whatever creative avenue they choose. For star athletes, it may be their sport. For musicians, it is their music. For artists, it is their craft. For your MASTERY game of Hide & Seek, it is your ability to find *You* and live your life connected to the unwavering flow of energy from God.

You are so much more than who you think you are—so much more than this physical body you call *me*. I like to imagine each of us as an iceberg. The visible tip above the waterline is our physical being, and the huge chunk of ice below the surface is our Spirit—our non-physical being—which is far greater than what we see or know in this reality we call life. You are always connected to the part of you that is below the surface of the water. You just may not be able to see it from your vantage point. An iceberg has the power to sink the largest ship in the world. Your power is just as incredible when you find—or connect with—the *You* that is hiding below the surface.

Give yourself the gift of acknowledging that you are far greater than what you can see with your physical eyes. Use the Universal Laws to fully embrace all of the possibilities your life has to offer. Play with the ideas of mental focus and connectedness, opposites and flow, and vibration and thought power. See how you can use what you know and the new possibilities of what you have yet to discover to achieve through alignment.

PART TWO

DISCOVERING YOUR TRUTH

CHAPTER SIX

SAVOR THE JOURNEY

*T*he S in MASTERY stands for *Savor the Journey*. Have you ever been so caught up in an experience that nothing else mattered? It may have been during a new relationship when you wanted nothing more than to be with that special person. It may have been when you were involved in a creative project that you couldn't stop thinking about. It may have been during an adventurous vacation when you were exploring your new surroundings. It may have even been when you were playing Hide & Seek as a child and your world was filled with the excitement and anticipation of the game! Whenever it was, take a moment to bring yourself back to the feeling of such an experience.

What word would you use to describe it? *Exhilarating, exciting, fun, fresh, alluring, enchanting?* This feeling brings a smile to my face just writing about it. There is a deeply rooted sense of fulfillment in such experiences. Why? Because in times like these, we are completely immersed in the present moment, and our awareness is focused on the joy of what is happening around us and within us. It is in these moments that you are one with the *You* in your MASTERY game of Hide & Seek. This is the essence of Savoring the Journey.

Realizing your potential for fulfillment in life is a game changer. This awareness is an *Olly Olly Oxen Free*—a game-changing moment when something major happens in the game and there is a noticeable switch in momentum. The momentum of feeling gratitude begins to build in your life: gratitude for the little things, for people, for opportunities, and for yourself. The more gratitude you have, the more fulfillment you will experience.

I used to say, "Enjoy the journey," but over time I have come to realize that using the word *enjoy* to describe the journey covers only one level. Defining how you take in your journey by using the word *savor* covers much more territory. We have the ability to look for a deeper meaning of satisfaction in every moment of our lives. The word *savor* is defined as "to taste or to enjoy completely." When you savor something, you are looking for the deeper meaning and complete enjoyment of it.

We have the ability to look for a deeper meaning
of satisfaction in every moment of our lives.

SWEET, SOUR, SALTY, BITTER, ASTRINGENT, AND PUNGENT

Savor is often used to define our experience of food or drinks. In the MASTERY game of Hide & Seek, I love looking at life's different experiences through the lens of how we taste our food—sweet, sour, salty, bitter, astringent, or pungent. According to the Chopra Center, ancient Ayurvedic teachings recommend eating foods representative of all six tastes at every meal to feel satisfied and ensure that all nutrients and major food groups are represented. This theory makes a lot of sense. It's a natural way for our bodies to be nourished by Mother Earth. There is a perfect balance of everything we need to be fulfilled nutritionally in nature.

Balance is the key to mastering this concept of savoring the journey. If you don't have the right balance, things feel "off." When you combine the six tastes together in the right balance, the food tastes delicious. On the other hand, too much of one type or a certain combination can taste awful.

Some combinations are winners across the board, like peanut butter and chocolate. Most of the tastes are actually represented in these two ingredients. This is one combo I keep in my book of "healthy" treats when I need a pick-me-up. Why? Because I savor it. Every bite brings me complete satisfaction and enjoyment. In fact, I usually know when it's time to stop (although it doesn't mean I always do) when I realize that the bite I just took doesn't taste as good as the bites before it. The intensity of fulfillment begins to fade because my body's nutritional needs have been met. After a while, the intensity will return and I can decide when to savor the treat again.

Just as we have the ability to savor a tasty treat, we can savor our experiences in life. Taking in the variety of flavors of a situation, appreciating the contrast, dreaming about how it could be even better, and feeling completely fulfilled and grateful are just some of the ways you can savor your journey. This world is filled with a richness and fullness to suit your palate in every way you can imagine. Finding the right blend, or discovering the perfect balance of a combination of tastes, is a part of your MASTERY games of Hide & Seek.

Personal Rulebook Play
TASTING THE RICHNESS
OF EVERY MOMENT

Do you have a favorite blend? Can you imagine how full your life would be if you began to appreciate the many tastes that come to you day by day? Take out your Personal Rulebook, and for the next two days, spend a few minutes writing down brief descriptions of the moments you were able to savor. This helps you to create an awareness of what is happening in your daily journey and the depth of how you are experiencing that journey. Then, ask yourself the following questions:

+ What are the various flavors of this situation?

+ What can I appreciate about any contrasting elements in this?

+ How could this experience be even better?

+ How can I completely savor and be grateful right now?

After the first two days of responding in your Personal Rulebook, just take a mental note of what is happening in any given moment and consciously take it in. It could be as simple as looking around the room and appreciating the color of paint on the walls, a smell in the room, the vibrancy of a plant, or just being thankful for the way you feel *right now.*

ACCESS YOUR ESSENCE

Once you begin to recognize—regularly—that every day is part of your life journey, you can start to have an appreciation for what that journey means to you. You can begin to savor it. You can begin to find the depth in every moment, however big or small it may be. Savoring your journey is an essential part of Discovering Your Truth in your MASTERY game of Hide & Seek. Your truth is your essence. For you to become a master of your life, you must embrace the essence of who you are.

Discovering Your Truth is one of the most freeing parts of the game, just like when you played Hide & Seek as a child. Remember how free you felt when you were playing the game? You weren't worried about whether you were playing the game right or wrong. You were just having fun, being yourself, and going with the moment—whatever it was. Today, this is the part where you again get to realize that nothing you do, feel, or say is wrong. This is the part where you get to discover that everything you have experienced has created who you are today and who you will become tomorrow. This is the part where you get to see the magnificence of all that you call *Me.* Ironically, it will be when you find the *You* in your MASTERY games that you will discover the truth of who *Me* really is.

One of the outcomes of Savor the Journey is confidence. When you are able to access the essence of who you are, you will naturally develop an enduring confidence that is deeply rooted and difficult to throw off. Remember that the word *confidence* comes from the root base *to confide*. Confidence is your ability to confide in and trust yourself. This deep confidence allows you to fully radiate and express who you are. Have you ever faced a decision and just known in your gut what the right answer was? Maybe it was a situation at work or it might have been a decision about a relationship. Whatever area of your life it was in, even without getting feedback from others or consulting with an expert, you had a deep knowing about what was right for you. This decision may have even been in contrast to what logically made the most sense or what would be considered most acceptable by others.

These are examples of Hide & Seek games where you are discovering what your truth really is. Your truth is just that—*yours*. So often we get lost in our lives because we are looking to outside influences and in the wrong areas for answers. Once you tap into the confidence that comes from understanding, you just can't get it wrong; you will feel a satisfaction that you may have only dreamed about before. Accessing your own essence is about reclaiming your innate internal joy and recommitting to that which inspires and uplifts your nature.

This access happens when you combine elements such as balance, discipline, and systemization with elements such as tenacity, productivity, and achievement. The first three elements offer a sense of center and groundedness, while the remaining three contribute to forward movement. When you combine these elements, they create a dynamic image of your essence as you explore your own personal odyssey. Your capacity to follow your bliss, or whatever resonates with you, brings your creative visions to fruition and produces genuine fulfillment and tangible results.

Here are some keys to understanding your essence and how to access it:

✦ Your essence is the Life Force within you *and* the unique physical qualities that make you, you.

✦ Your essence is dynamic. Just like the concept of polarities discussed in Chapter 5: Achieve through Alignment, your essence is a constantly flowing energy in your life.

✦ Your essence is always peaceful, loving, open, passionate, grounded, and curious.

✦ Your essence is the very nature of who you are at the most basic, yet profound, level.

Personal Rulebook Play
ACCESSING MY ESSENCE

Grab your Personal Rulebook. In this Play, you are going to practice accessing your own essence. Begin by thinking about your answers to the following questions, then jot down your thoughts:

✦ What makes you special or unique? What words would you use to describe you? Zero in on what you do that makes other people want to connect with you. What makes you different? What are you good at?

✦ Can you see how this dynamic energy plays in your life? How do you feel when you are connected with your essence compared to when you are overthinking something in your head?

✦ When do you feel the most calm, grounded, and at peace?

✦ Have you ever had a moment when you felt a profound level of connection with your soul? What were you doing? What made that moment so special?

Next, the best way I have found to access my essence is to do things I savor! When we are purely appreciating whatever we may be doing, we are accessing the essence of who we are. So, what is it you love to do? Answer the following questions in your rulebook:

✦ Write down five to ten things you love doing.

✦ How can you do *at least* one of those things every day?

✦ Make a commitment to yourself. Set the intention to fully radiate, express, and honor who you really are. Write down two ways you will remind yourself to access and honor *You*.

Now, build your ability to access your essence with the following affirmations:

✦ "I am a vital, joyful, and grounded person."

✦ "I feel connected to the very nature of who I am."

✦ "I love the dynamic energy that is *Me*."

THE KEY TO EVERYTHING

There are moments in life when you know you can never go back to the way you lived prior to that moment. When I learned what I am about to share with you, it was like I started playing my MASTERY games of Hide & Seek with a supercharged flashlight. It was such a shift in the way I had been thinking about life that my entire world changed forever.

Let me just preface this by saying that I have always been an achiever. Someone who is constantly looking to do more, be more, and accomplish more. In my quest to do-do-do, I often didn't enjoy what I was doing. I was simply doing the task to get to the end result. This attitude will certainly help you achieve what you want, but it can also leave a path of destruction. It's like you're a hurricane barreling through, and after you're done, there's a mess to clean up.

In my life, this mess looked like a strained relationship with my husband because I was constantly on my computer and disconnected with my family. It looked like many trips to the chiropractor and massage therapist because my body was so filled with physical stress from my constant "go mode." It looked like always feeling that there is something else I need to be doing and never feeling fulfilled because something was weighing on my mind.

One day I was listening to some spiritual teachings from Abraham-Hicks on YouTube and heard the following message: "Don't do the work for the manifestation. Do the work for the feeling and the manifestation will follow." I must've been primed and ready because this message was a sudden insight—a true Olly Olly Oxen Free—that changed the way I lived my life. What I understood for the first time in my life, at that moment, was that our lives are about savoring the moment. Yes, it is great to achieve our goals, but the goal is not the primary reason we are doing the work. The primary reason we are doing the work is to *feel* good while we are doing it! Did you hear that? The primary reason you are doing the work is to feel good while you are doing it. That feeling allows everything in your life to begin to flow. It is the tangible evidence of all the Universal Laws covered in Chapter 5: Achieve through Alignment.

> *The primary reason you are doing the work*
> *is to feel good while you are doing it.*

I say this awareness is the key to everything because **it is the key to everything!** If you will start to live your life knowing that your primary focus is to feel good while you are doing whatever it is you need to do, your life will change forever. I speak this so confidently because I have been living it myself. I live it even when I'm doing eighteen things around my house and I start to have a little voice in my head say, "Why didn't my family put these dishes in the dishwasher?" or "I've got to get dinner started and I just finished working a full day." When I used to have those thoughts, I could go off on a tangent in my mind, and watch out! By the time my family members walked into the room, they would either get an earful or they would feel the tension in the room because I was stressed out and, at times, even ticked off.

Now, instead of allowing that thought to initiate a negative internal dialogue with myself, I instead stop and think about why I want to do the task at hand. I think, *It makes me so happy to have a clean kitchen.* I think, *I'm so glad I am able to be a successful businesswoman and a great wife and mom.* This doesn't mean that I won't remind my kids and hubby to put their dishes in the dishwasher (which happens regularly at my house) or that I won't decide to order takeout instead of cooking a meal. What it does mean is that I don't waste my time thinking negative thoughts, feeling stressed, and simply not enjoying my life. I am happier. My family is happier because they aren't walking into a hurricane. And life feels so much easier.

This is all because I have learned to make a conscious shift. I've decided to remember that it is *not* the fact that my kitchen is clean that will ultimately create lasting fulfillment in my life. It is the fact that I am feeling good throughout my day that will give me lasting fulfillment. I've learned that when I follow the advice, "Do the work for the feeling and the manifestation will follow," my kitchen does stay cleaner because everyone else in the house knows it's important to me and they want to do their part to help me out. No more arguments, no more personal frustration, no more "Mom just lost it" moments. Let me be really clear here: I am not saying that I am never out of balance and have become the "perfect" woman, but the awareness that I have 100 percent control over my thoughts and how I choose to experience my activities has given me the power to choose what feels good rather than choose what doesn't.

This choose-what-feels-good perspective can be applied to any area of your life. I just gave you my personal mom example, but this concept is just as easily applied at the office. If you are approaching your day because you have a task to do and getting it finished is your only objective, you may get it done, but what are the ramifications if you don't feel good while you're doing it? Are you kind to your coworkers when you are not feeling good? Are you doing your best work when you are not feeling good? Are you making good food choices when you don't feel good?

The key to savoring—truly savoring—every moment and soaking up every bit of fulfillment from your life is to stop focusing on the manifestation or outcome you want and start focusing on feeling good while you do the work toward the manifestation. Then, if the outcome is different from what you anticipated (or if it never arrives), you will still be fulfilled because you enjoyed your experience along the way. And I think you will find that even if your original outcome doesn't happen, what does manifest will be even better.

Personal Rulebook Play
FEELING GOOD IN MY LIFE

Get our your Personal Rulebook, and begin this Play by setting an intention to start feeling good in your life. Also make an intention to try to "catch yourself" when you aren't feeling good about things. Write these intentions in your rulebook.

Now, think about ways to start feeling good while doing the things in life you need to do. If you realize you are stressed about something, ask yourself, "Why is this important to me?" See if you can approach the situation from a different angle. Answer the following questions:

✦ Is there someone else who can do it?

✦ Is there something that would make it more enjoyable?

✦ Can you mentally change your perspective to help you enjoy what you're doing?

Make an effort to do something positive to help you shift to a new state of mind or state of being. If you are having trouble changing your perspective, stop the activity you are doing and do something enjoyable and good for you for a few minutes. For example, take a ten-minute break to watch a funny video or go for a quick walk outside. You could call someone you love (but rather than complain about what's happening, talk to that person about all the things you love about him or her). Taking a nap works, too. Whatever it may be for you that will help you feel better, try it. But keep in mind that heading for the alcohol or junk food machine would not be a positive action to take.

FOCUS ON YOUR STRENGTHS

Where your focus goes energy flows is a fact you have come to understand. It doesn't matter whether you're paying attention to all the things going wrong in your life or you're feeling gratitude for the many blessings you experience every day. You also know that the frequency of your thoughts affects what you do, as well as who and what comes into your life. With that in mind, it is now time to turn your attention back to your strengths that we explored during your second Personal Rulebook Play in Chapter 2: The Rules. Remember, we are each born with innate gifts, and you will have these strengths from the day you are born until the day you die. As you focus your attention on these strengths, you can become a master of you. This is the expression of personal mastery at its finest.

Knowing and focusing on your strengths applies to your MASTERY game of Hide & Seek and brilliantly fits right into the Discover Your Truth portion of the game! Your strengths are part of your truth. Your strengths are the physical representations of who you are. Your strengths help you get to know yourself better . . . and even more important, they help you appreciate yourself more.

> *Your strengths help you get to know yourself better . . . and*
> *even more important, they help you appreciate yourself more.*

As a brief refresher, the following rules will help you recognize your strengths so that you can focus on activities that play to them. When you are playing to your strengths:

✦ You lose track of time.

✦ You feel energized.

✦ You don't want to stop doing the activity.

✦ You can't wait to get back to the activity.

✦ It strengthens you and you feel empowered.

If you are doing things in life that you may be good at, but those things deplete you, then they are not your innate and natural strengths. For me, when I focus my attention on activities that drain me, it is very clear that I have steered away from my strengths. I feel stressed out and tired all the time. Through my Hide & Seek games, I have been able to see that while I may be good at what I'm doing, I am completely draining myself and leaving a path of destruction when all was said and done. Remember that hurricane we talked about earlier? Yep, Hurricane Karri at it again.

Personal Rulebook Playback
MY STRENGTHS

Grab your Personal Rulebook and revisit your second Play. Without looking at your original answers, respond to each of the questions below in your rulebook. Knowing what you know now, do you think you will answer any of these questions differently? Let's see.

Depleting Activities

✦ Can you think about activities in your life that you may be good at, but that leave you feeling drained?

✦ What are these activities?

✦ What is it about these activities that drains you?

✦ What is the "cost" to you for keeping these activities in your life? Your relationships? Your energy? Your happiness?

✦ How could you adjust your approach to delegate, or eliminate, these activities from your life?

Strengthening Activities

✦ Can you think about activities that strengthen you, that you are good at, and that leave you feeling energized?

✦ What do you enjoy most about these activities?

✦ How do you feel they strengthen you when you do them?

✦ What are the benefits you experience?

✦ What are the benefits others experience when you are playing to your strengths?

✦ How can you spend more of your time playing to your strengths in your life? At work? At home?

Think about how you can, as well as why you would want to, focus more of your attention on your strengths. Creating a reason for and seeing the value in doing something is a major step in feeling motivated and changing your behavior. New behaviors can lead to a happier life and help you savor your journey.

BECOME A POWER POSER

When you are savoring your journey, you are appreciating all the aspects of your life. This means exploring the literally countless things you can put your attention on. If you get to the root reason of why anybody does anything, it is because they believe it will make them feel good. Feeling good is, ultimately, what we all want. In my opinion, one of the most satisfying aspects to put your attention on is understanding how to feel good.

In my own life, I have discovered that feeling good comes from feeling empowered. Feeling empowered can be experienced in many ways. This may mean physically challenging yourself, as an athlete does in his or her given sport, or it may mean feeling confident in who you are and not worrying about what others think of you. Whatever *empowered* may mean to you at this point in your life, feeling empowered will enhance your ability to savor your journey in a way that just feels good.

Have you ever noticed there seems to be a spiral effect when things are going right or wrong in your life? For example, when you want to be healthier and lose weight, you start working out, which makes you want to eat healthier. You start to sleep better and you make all-around healthier choices in your life. You begin to feel really good about yourself and you have a more positive outlook on everything in your life.

Have you ever experienced a scenario like this? Or maybe it was the opposite? For example, you have been doing great on your healthy lifestyle plan and you decide you're just not up to working out, or you have obligations that prohibit you from getting your movement in for a few days. During those days, you become more lax about what you are putting in your body and opt for pizza and cupcakes with less water intake. It feels like over the course of just a few days you begin to feel disappointed in your choices and think you've lost all of the progress you made as your thoughts take a turn down "Negative Nellie" Avenue.

Through the lessons learned in Chapter 5: Achieve through Alignment, you now know this is not just a perception that you are spiraling up or down the scale. This is the result of the Universal Laws working in your life—just as they unwaveringly and always do. Thankfully, you also now know what these laws are and how you can use them to empower yourself along your journey. The reason for this spiral effect is explained most simply through the Law of Attraction. When you start to operate on a certain frequency, your thoughts, feelings, and actions line up. This means your body, mind, and spirit are all aligned. So if you want to make a shift in frequency, start by focusing on one area and trust that the others will follow.

A fun and easy way to do this in your everyday life is to become a power poser. A what? Yep, you read it right, *a power poser!* If you want some hard facts and don't like just hearing about the unseen forces of the universe, this one's for you. One day I received an email with a link to a TED talk by Amy Cuddy, an Associate Professor of Business Administration in the Negotiation, Organizations & Markets Unit at Harvard Business School. At Harvard, they decided to study the physiological effects (meaning what measurable changes happen in the body) of posing in different positions. They chose what they call high power poses and low power poses. The high power poses are basically standing or sitting in a position where you are open and big. The low power poses are standing or sitting in a position where you are closed and small. (Take a look at the figure on the following page for a visual.)

One by one, the researchers assigned each participant either the high power poses or the low power poses, and asked them to stand or sit in one of the five options for two minutes. The participants were not given any information. They were simply asked to stand or sit in one of the positions offered. Researchers took a saliva sample from each participant before and after the two minutes to measure levels of cortisol (the stress hormone) and testosterone (the "I can do it" hormone).

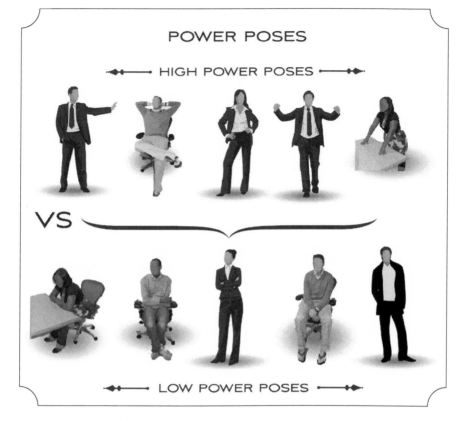

The results were clear. Testosterone went up and cortisol went down in the high power poses, and the inverse happened in the low power poses. So when people are open and big with their body, they increase their "I can do it" hormone and decrease their stress levels. When people are physically closed and small, they increase their stress levels and decrease their confidence levels.

What does this mean to you? It means that the spiral effect can be used to your advantage when you want to feel empowered. When you are in what I call a "power state," your body and mind are aligned, which will help you create the experience you desire. It means you have the power to control how you experience your life. Power posing is a tool you can use to step into your own power and feel appreciation on a regular basis.

Personal Rulebook Play
POWER POSING

Get out your Personal Rulebook. This Play is all about the application of high power poses. Jot down any notes you want to remember from the Play, but don't forget to get out there and practice your power poses. Here are some practice situations:

If you are in a crummy mood and want to change it:

Power posing for as few as two minutes changes your physiological response, which can then change your mind's focus as well as your mood.

If you are about to go into an appointment and need to be on your A-game:

Power posing for as few as two minutes increases your "I can do it" hormone and decrease your stress hormone, helping you to feel confident and in control.

If you find yourself consistently taking a passive or submissive role in a certain area of your life that is not serving you and you want to step into your power:

Practice power posing when you are alone and visualize yourself being more assertive and bold. When you find yourself in the recurring type of situation where you feel passive/submissive, subtly move your body into a power pose and focus your attention on becoming stronger in that moment. It may take you a little while to get the hang of it, but you can do it! You will even have the testosterone results to prove it. (Ha-ha!)

For more on this Harvard study, watch the YouTube video I mentioned above. Go to YouTube and search "Amy Cuddy Power Poser." Ironically, the title of this clip is *Game Changer: Amy Cuddy, Power Poser Game Changer!* See, this is just another Olly Olly Oxen Free opportunity within your MASTERY game of Hide & Seek!

THE *WHY NOT?* ATTITUDE

I had the pleasure of diving into this idea of savoring the journey during the writing of this chapter. For me, teaching something without personal experience feels empty and disconnected. To share with you the possibilities of savoring your journey, I must have a personal reference as proof it can be done. This belief is supported by an attitude that has been with me for most of my life. That attitude is one of openness to something new, willingness to try something different, and courage to explore the potential outcomes and possibilities.

Many years ago I was talking to my mom about the idea of traveling to Germany to visit a guy I'd met in passing on a cruise; we had been emailing each other for a couple of months and I was smitten with him. For me, it was exciting to think about traveling to a new country to see him and to do something that sounded fun and a little crazy. I'll never forget my mom's response when I shared my idea for the trip.

She paused and replied, "Why would you want to do that?"

I answered, "Why not?"

I didn't end up traveling to Germany for a variety of reasons, but this question and my reply got me thinking. What is the basis of how we are choosing to live our lives? For instance, do you ask yourself, "Why would I do that?" with the intention of talking yourself out of something? Or when you ask, "Why would I do that?" are you looking for all the reasons *to* do it? I am not suggesting you throw caution to the wind and do things that don't feel right to you, but it is certainly liberating to throw in a "Why not?" during the deliberation process.

As I have coached people over the years, I have discovered there are people who tend to look for all the reasons to make something happen, and there are people who want to make sure they have looked at all of the possibilities and potential downfalls. Each of these approaches is common and just part of the individual's process and mind-set. But when it comes to a situation where you really want to do something and it feels good deep down inside, you will experience more joy and fulfillment when you approach it with a "Why not?" attitude. For example, maybe you've always wanted to learn how to salsa dance. What's held you back from finding a class and joining it? If the tone of your "Why not?" leads you to all the reasons *not* to do it, you are likely coming up with answers like:

- My kids need me.

- I'm too tired.

- I don't have the time.

- I don't want to take the class alone.

If the tone of your "Why not?" is about finding all the reasons *to* take salsa lessons, you are more likely to come up with answers such as:

- I can be an example to my kids to never stop learning.

- I can get in better shape through my dance classes.

- I can carve out extra hours in my week by getting help from others and cutting out some time in front of the television.

- This could be a great way to have some fun with my spouse or a friend who wants to join me, or I'll meet other salsa enthusiasts and make some new friends in the class.

The purpose of asking "Why not?" in your MASTERY game of Hide & Seek is to help you Discover Your Truth. When you discover what holds you back from going after your dreams and experiencing your life to the fullest extent possible, you learn more about who you are and who you want to be. This MASTERY game is finding the *You* within that has no fear and is curious about all that life has to offer. By asking yourself "What is holding me back in this situation?" you are able to discover what feels good to you and what makes you happy because you are willing to take a look at the reasons you may be holding yourself back.

In my personal experience and through coaching, I have found a variety of reasons we choose to forego the "Why not?" attitude. Lack of mental clarity, lack of confidence, personal beliefs, and fear about the unknown are the major culprits that hold us back from truly savoring our experience in this lifetime. These mental states are the primary causes for passing on joy, fun, and excitement that is just waiting for you if you are willing to say, "Why not?"

It is in times of challenge, confusion, or uncertainty that you are given your greatest opportunities to Discover Your Truth! When you choose to play a MASTERY game of Hide & Seek with yourself and go looking for the *You* that is hiding within any given situation, you are becoming more grounded, more focused, and you develop a sense of clarity about who you are and what you want in your life. It is through this profound self-exploration that you find personal satisfaction, fulfillment, and deeply rooted self-confidence—a profound self-exploration that begins with two simple words: "Why not?"

Personal Rulebook Play
HOW MY INTENTIONS AFFECT MY DECISIONS

In this Play, you will be taking a closer look at your intentions when you are making decisions about taking an action in your life. Are you looking for reasons to avoid, or are you looking for reasons to move forward? Pull out your Personal Rulebook and think about a situation in which you were challenged, felt confused, or maybe you were even excited, then respond to the following:

✦ Where did you initially go in your thought process as you thought about your options?

✦ Did you look for the pros or the cons?

◆ Did you find yourself looking to others for answers, or going within to see what felt best about the situation?

◆ How did you feel after you made a decision? (Whether that decision was to move full-steam ahead, or to pull back and wait.)

◆ Why did you feel that way?

◆ Do you feel that you were true to yourself?

◆ Do you feel that you honored the voice inside you? Do you feel that you gave away your power by doing what others wanted rather than listening to your own truth?

PUTTING THE CHERRY ON TOP

Now that you have had an opportunity to learn different elements about how you can savor your journey, what are you going to do to take that first bite? How can you Discover Your Truth by savoring every morsel that comes your way? You have so much power within you, and as you begin to appreciate the tastes of every situation in your life, you begin to develop your own palate.

You now know how to gain access to your own essence: that truth that feels right to you. That truth that unlocks your power. Realizing that the key that unlocks your power is doing what feels good and right to you will help you develop the self-confidence needed to become a master. A master knows his or her strengths and uses them wisely. A master knows what can hold him or her back and chooses to explore the opportunity with curiosity—just like you used to do when you were a child playing Hide & Seek in your neighborhood.

You are one step closer to becoming a master of your own life as you learn to feel gratitude for all that you encounter day to day. Truly taking in everything about your experience, savoring the moments, will allow you to find satisfaction that you may have only dreamed about before. Remember, even the bitter or pungent tastes have a purpose in your life. When you add them into the entire recipe, you end up with a delectable masterpiece that you can savor time and time again.

CHAPTER SEVEN

THINK WITH COMPASSION

*T*hinking with compassion—the *T* in *MASTERY*—is the second part of Discovering Your Truth. By embracing your essence and savoring all that makes you the outstanding and amazing being that you are, you take the first step in the discovery of your truth. The second part of finding your truth is learning to integrate the dynamic polar opposites that lie within you. These opposites give you the ability to accept yourself as well as others and to experience the fullness within any given situation.

What does it mean to integrate your polar opposites? In the case of Think with Compassion, it means integrating your masculine and feminine qualities to create a sum that is greater than the two parts. Whether we are male or female, we have both masculine and feminine characteristics. These characteristics each bring great strengths and inherent challenges as we navigate through our daily lives. It is when you can use both qualities in a supportive way that you unlock the truth of who you are and live in fulfillment.

Let's briefly review what we learned in Chapter 5: Achieve through Alignment about masculine and feminine essences:

Masculine = Dynamic   Feminine = Magnetic

The feminine essence embodies magnetic and receptive abilities. The outward expressions show up as love, patience, and intuition. The feminine has a gentle and quiet, yet profoundly powerful, nature to it. The power of the feminine nature has the ability to literally draw you in.

The masculine essence shows up as dynamic and initiatory. The outward expressions of the masculine essence are logic, dynamic energy, and self-reliance. These elements have an intense and forceful power. They make things happen. They get stuff done. They are big and swift.

You have the full spectrum of both of these essences within you. As you are able to recognize the qualities of the masculine and feminine essences, and use them appropriately, you will be able to achieve a level of personal mastery in your life. The ability to consciously do this starts with the skill of awareness. I personally learned the power of the masculine and feminine over the course of about a year. During that year, the concept of masculine and feminine qualities came into my life from various avenues. It came in through my personal growth work with one of my coaches. It came to me through a nine-month alchemy class that I attended. And it came to me through another inspirational speaker at an event I attended.

Learning this powerful information about the difference between masculine and feminine energies, and discovering that I was primarily living my life in an energy that was *not* my true nature was a huge eye-opener. What does that mean? It means that while I am a woman who is primarily feminine (although there are a small percentage of women who truly are masculine, most are feminine), I was living the majority of my life using my masculine qualities. The outcomes of that choice—to name just a few—were more mental and physical stress, a strained relationship with my husband, and great success in business. As I began to recognize the plusses and minuses of living primarily in my masculine energy, I began to rethink the manner in which I wanted to live my life. Great success may sound like a positive, but I began to realize that great success in business at the expense of personal failure in my relationship was not a worthwhile trade. I also learned how I could use my masculine power to be successful at work *and* use my feminine power to be equally successful at home. Win-win! *Ding, ding, ding!* It was like winning the jackpot in Vegas.

Here's the deal. The bottom line is that when you are a masculine man living your life primarily in your feminine, or a feminine woman living primarily in your masculine, you are making your life more difficult rather than living in the flow and feeling an internal sense of freedom.

A brief note here: As I stated before, a small percentage of men are truly feminine, and women are truly masculine. And that small percentage does not relate to sexuality. There are heterosexual and homosexual women who are masculine, while most are feminine. The same idea also applies to gay and straight men. Whether someone operates primarily from masculine or feminine energy is not related to sexual orientation, but gauged by innate qualities. Masculine qualities are typically categorized as dynamic, and feminine qualities categorized as magnetic.

So how do you know if you are living in the flow? How do you know what masculine is and what feminine is? As you look around you, and if we go back through the ages, you will find many examples of the masculine and feminine energies. Earlier when I shared the Law of Gender, I shared how the masculine and feminine show up in almost everything we experience from humans to plants to animals to electrons and magnetic poles. The poles of magnets provide a visual example of how these contrasting energies interact with one another. These differences show up in personalities, in nature, and in our physical bodies.

Initially, it can be difficult for some to grasp exactly what "dynamic masculine" and "magnetic feminine" mean. I have found that there are a few easy ways to think about this concept. The first way is fairly obvious. By simply looking at men and women throughout history, you will generally find that women have been the nurturers and men have been the hunters. Women have sexual magnetism, and men are driven to take action and achieve. Women have a soft and gentle nature about them, and men are tough. While these are generalizations, they help us envision clear examples of what is masculine and what is feminine.

Another way to recognize the difference between these two energies is to use the metaphor of the head and the heart. The head represents the masculine, and the heart represents the feminine. Your head is logical (not emotional), thinks in a linear fashion, and wants to strategically solve problems. In contrast, your heart is sensitive, intuitive, and solves problems by feeling the solution rather than analyzing. These "characteristics" are a few examples of how the dynamic masculine is represented by the head and the magnetic feminine is represented by the heart.

Looking at ancient traditions, you find the masculine/feminine energies represented as well. According to the Pachamama Alliance, *The Eagle and the Condor* is an ancient Amazon prophecy that speaks of human societies splitting into two paths—that of the Eagle and that of the Condor. The path of the Condor is the path of heart, intuition, and the feminine. The path of the Eagle is the path of the mind, the industrial, and the masculine.

When you begin to see how the Law of Gender plays out in your life, you can use it to reach another level of personal mastery. Understanding that you have both masculine and feminine qualities and knowing how you use those qualities in your relationships, your actions, and your thoughts can be a game changer. Being able to spend most of your time in your primary energy will give you unlimited power and an internal feeling of ease as you go through each day. When you are trying to be someone you are not or you are trying to act in a way that doesn't feel natural to you, it is extremely stressful and draining.

Think about a time in your life when you were pretending to be something you were not. How did you feel? What physical, emotional, and mental toll did it take on you? If and when you chose a more authentic position, did you feel a sense of freedom? Did it feel like a weight had been lifted from you? As a coach, it is so common to hear a client say, "I feel like such a huge weight has been lifted off my shoulders," when the client has chosen to step into her own power and stop pretending to be someone else.

Discovering Your Truth means understanding, knowing, and accepting yourself just as you are. When you accept and embrace who you are, you give yourself the gift of worthiness. Feeling worthy —feeling that you deserve to live whatever life you choose to live—is one of the most freeing choices you will ever make. Once you believe that you are worthy to do, to be, or to have whatever your heart desires, you begin to allow true happiness and abundance into your life. Part of that discovery starts with accepting and consciously integrating your masculine and feminine energies into your life.

Once you believe that you are worthy to do, to be,
or to have whatever your heart desires, you begin to
allow true happiness and abundance into your life.

Personal Rulebook Play
MY PRIMARY ENERGY

This Personal Rulebook Play is about gaining awareness about your primary energy and how it shows up in your life. This is not a time to pass judgment on yourself or others, but rather a chance for you to start understanding how this powerful duality of masculine and feminine plays a role in your life. Grab your rulebook, ponder the following questions, and then jot down your responses:

What are the qualities of your primary energy?

✦ Do you spend most of your time in your masculine or feminine energy?

✦ How has that energy served you in your personal life? In your professional life?

- If you have a spouse or life partner, what is your partner's primary energy? Does that seem to be where your partner spends the most time?

- Can you see how your energies complement or clash?

- Do you see how your interactions change when you are in your masculine or feminine?

COMPASSIONATE POWER™

During my "aha" moment regarding the masculine and feminine dynamics, I came up with a phrase that encompasses both energies: Compassionate Power™. Along my journey of self-discovery—my MASTERY game of Hide & Seek—I realized I was a feminine woman living primarily in my masculine energy. Once I recognized the power both energies possessed, I was able to see how they could each serve me in the greatest way.

Masculine and feminine energies each possess a power that is immensely strong yet very different. On a sliding scale, the word I believe best represents the feminine end of the scale is *empathy*. The word that best represents the masculine end of the scale is *domination*. While other qualities fill the space between those opposites, these two qualities are the bookends.

Compassionate Power™ is learning the balance between empathy and domination. For some, that may mean stepping into their power and out of their empathic comfort zone. For others it may mean pulling their energy inward to feel their way through a situation. Compassionate Power™ is about learning the balance between living from your head and your heart. It's about using your masculine and feminine energies synergistically.

The Power Scale

Domination ⟵——— Compassionate Power™ ———⟶ Empathy

The feminine side of the power scale is about emotional integrity. When one masters emotional integrity, he or she is able to honestly and responsibly express feelings. Emotional authenticity is key in order to step into your personal feminine power. Within some of your MASTERY games of Hide & Seek, your role is to develop a constant practice of owning your feelings and expressing them without blame or judgment.

Those who live in the range of "extreme empathy," however, can be taken advantage of. A good friend of mine describes it as being a "limp noodle." Allowing yourself to be taken advantage of by others is not the purest form of empathy. Empathy in its purest form means stepping into your feminine power. Feminine power means:

⬩ Allowing your feelings to lead you

⬩ Communicating accurately and openly

⬩ Not using your feelings to attack others

⬩ Not apologizing for your feelings

When these traits become the basis of your power, you feel a sense of clarity, a firm footing, and a knowing that only comes from this powerful emotional authenticity. When you are living in this way, you feel a determination to express yourself accurately in your thoughts, words, and actions. Feminine power is profoundly strong, and whether you are a woman or a man, the ability to go to this energy when you need it is the skill of a master. It would be a misperception to assume that feminine energy is used only by women. Men are missing the boat if they do not acknowledge the power they could possess if they would embrace the empathetic side of the scale. If we look at the earlier example of Nelson Mandela in Chapter 5: Achieve through Alignment, we can see the power of the feminine at work in his life. He wouldn't have amassed millions to follow his lead if he had not been authentic in his feelings, words, and actions. This was a man who understood how to honestly and responsibly express his feelings and effectively communicate with emotional integrity. This is feminine power!

While Nelson Mandela was able to step into this empathic power when he needed to, he was also fiercely passionate about his cause and had a dominating drive to achieve his desired outcome. This masculine energy allowed him to take action and move others into action.

The masculine side of the power scale is about emotional desire. When one masters emotional desire, he or she is able to simultaneously move forward and let go. Detached desire is needed to step into your masculine power. This means that it is important for you to have strong desires. Those desires are what will give you the strength, energy, and drive to realize your goals. At the same time, it is also important to maintain a level of detachment from those desires. By not allowing yourself to be too "caught up" emotionally with your desires, you are able to have a level of objectivity that will ultimately help you achieve your goals.

> *It is important for you to have strong desires.*
> *Those desires are what will give you the strength,*
> *energy, and drive to realize your goals.*

Within your MASTERY games of Hide & Seek, your ability to create a practice to have the capacity to simultaneously move forward and let go will help you with the masculine part of thinking with compassion. Those with extreme domination tendencies are dictators. That is not the purest form of masculine energy. Domination in its purest form means stepping into your masculine power. Masculine power means:

- Allowing your desires to lead you
- Taking action authentically and ethically
- Honoring differences and looking for win-win solutions
- Cultivating your desires while being willing to let go when necessary

When these traits become the basis of your power, you feel a sense of clarity, strength, and motivation to move forward. You feel a determination to make things happen through your thoughts, words, and actions. Masculine power is strong, and just as it is with feminine power—whether you are a woman or a man—the ability to go to this energy when you need it is the skill of a master.

If we look at Nelson Mandela from the perspective of his ability to step into his masculine power, we see action, we see strength to engage millions of people who followed his lead, and we see immense passion and drive. Without his masculine power, his cause would have been a more personal endeavor that did not have the potential to influence so many others.

When these two powers are combined, Compassionate Power™ is the outcome. These two energies create the whole you, making it possible for you to find the singular *You* that is hiding in your MASTERY games of Hide & Seek. That is when you are able to reach your fullest potential.

Stepping into these powerful forces as you need them throughout your day will give you a sense of exhilaration that comes only from being in the flow with all that you are. Compassionate Power™ made it possible for Nelson Mandela to change himself . . . to change a country . . . to change the world.

Personal Rulebook Play
MY FEMININE AND MASCULINE POWER

Get out your Personal Rulebook. Revisit the Play in which you gained awareness of your primary energy, which energy you spend most of your time in, how those habits are serving you, and how they are translating into your relationships at home and work.

Now with your better understanding of the purest form of each energy, think about how you use masculine power and feminine power in your life. Remember, as you ponder and answer these questions, you do not need to judge or blame. Mastering the skill of Think with Compassion begins with feeling compassion for yourself.

If you don't believe you have been expressing your energies in their purest forms, look at it as an opportunity to expand into a more complete and authentic you! For children, compassion comes naturally. Go back to the innocence and self-acceptance you had as a kid when you were playing Hide & Seek with your friends. This feeling of personal freedom will give you the ability to access the best of both sides of you.

Feminine Power

✦ Do you allow your feelings to lead you?

✦ Do you communicate accurately and openly?

✦ Do you use your feelings to attack others?

✦ Do you apologize for your feelings?

Masculine Power

✦ Do you allow your desires to lead you?

✦ Do you take action authentically and ethically?

✦ Do you honor your differences and look for a solution for the greater good of all involved or do you attack others?

✦ Are you willing to face and experience your desires while being willing to let go when necessary?

Integration of Masculine and Feminine

Now you have an even deeper understanding about how you use these powerful forces. The final step in thinking with compassion is learning how to combine your masculine and feminine energies and integrate them into your life.

When you have mastered the ability to integrate these two energies in a balanced way you are living from a place of Compassionate Power™. Having the right balance, in any given moment, of self-nurturance and nurturance of others will bring you the greatest joy as you move through each day. This integration gives you the ability to accurately express the internal feelings you are experiencing. It also allows you to communicate your feelings from a place of emotional integrity and from a place of trust rather than control.

Sometimes we can get stuck in the habit of staying in one energy too often. Whether your primary energy is masculine or feminine, you have to move along the sliding scale of domination to empathy to find your truth and experience your full power. Getting stuck on one side of the scale might feel like discontentment or frustration or anxiety.

Whether your primary energy is masculine or feminine, you have to move along the sliding scale of domination to empathy to find your truth and experience your full power.

For example, a manager is stuck in the habit of always defaulting to his masculine energy, he will try to take action to create the outcome he wants. He may think, think, think until he is overwhelmed or confused. (Having thoughts is taking action.) He may try one way after another to try to "make it happen." He may enlist others, whether they want to help or not, to achieve his outcome. This is not to say that these behaviors will not lead him to some success, but these methods alone may not yield him the same success that he would enjoy if he allowed the magnetic feminine energy to also help his cause. And even if he does produce the same success, he may find that on the dynamic-masculine-only path to success, he experiences discontent, frustration, or anxiety.

To get even more specific, let's say this manager wants to increase his bottom line so that he can reach a higher bonus level for himself and his department. While the manager's intentions are to bring more abundance to his company, his subordinates, and himself, if he defaults to only his masculine energy to achieve the goal, he will likely experience resistance. That resistance may come in the form of employees who don't buy into his game plan. It may come in the form of stress because things are not happening in the way he believes they should be happening. That resistance might even be his lack of patience with his family or coworkers because he is feeling anxiety about achieving a goal that is not 100 percent in his control.

If this same manager chose to find more balance and step into his Compassionate Power™, he might discover that using some of his magnetic-feminine energy would help him achieve his goal in an easier and more enjoyable way. He would be able to clearly communicate his authentic and sincere desire to increase productivity so that everyone involved achieved a level of personal and professional success. His nurturing feminine energy would know how to connect with his team so that they, too, believed in his mission. He would not apologize for feeling the pressure that may come along during the process of reaching his objectives, and he would also be able to refrain from attacking others when he was feeling anxiety or frustration. These feminine qualities, in addition to his innate masculine "get the job done" qualities would create a synergy that is far more powerful than either energy on its own.

Personal Rulebook Play
CREATING COMPASSIONATE POWER

How can you integrate your masculine and feminine energy to create Compassionate Power™ in your life? Pull out your Personal Rulebook and think about a situation—now or in the past—where you have encountered feelings of frustration, discontent, or anxiety. Write down a brief (one to four sentences only) description of the situation and why you feel (or felt) stuck.

Write down which energy you are using when you are getting stuck. Do you see a pattern? Is one energy showing up more in these instances? Review the questions for both feminine power and masculine power in the previous Play to help you determine whether or not you are operating from the purest form of your feminine and masculine energies in this situation.

Now think about how you can move along the sliding scale of empathy to domination and see if you can add in some other qualities that will help to balance out the way you are approaching the situation.

THE HEAD-HEART CONTINUUM

One final tool that may help you integrate your masculine and feminine energies is to use what I call the Head-Heart Continuum. As we explored earlier, one way to grasp the concept of masculine and feminine energy is to use the metaphor of your head and heart. Your head represents your logical, linear, and strategic masculine energy. Your heart represents your sensitive, intuitive, and feeling feminine energy.

Your power resides in your ability to continually move, fluidly, from one to the other as you go through your day. Being comfortable and knowing how to access each of the energies when you need them is the key to mastering the skill of thinking with compassion. Imagine a continuum that looks like a figure eight with the top of it around your head, and the bottom of it around your heart. It is designed so that you can continuously follow that continuum and stay as long—or as quickly—as needed in either hemisphere. Most important, remember that for you to embody your full potential and power, you must be continuously moving, or flowing, around the continuum.

Personal Rulebook Play
STEPPING INTO MASCULINE
AND FEMININE ENERGIES

Get out your Personal Rulebook. In this Play, you will practice stepping into your masculine and feminine energies to help yourself in a challenging area of your life. This Play involves creative visualization, but feel free to jot down any ideas or thoughts that arise afterward in your rulebook.

Stepping into Feminine Energy

The nurturing gifts you are about to give yourself are sometimes easier to do when you envision yourself as a child. Whether you were given this reassurance by a parent or caregiver in your real childhood or not, you can reach back in time and change who you are today by accessing your feminine energy and nurturing yourself. For some, it is difficult to nurture themselves because they feel it is selfish or that they don't deserve it. Even if you feel that way, I encourage you to give it a try.

Once you have read the example below, close your eyes and spend a few minutes reconnecting with yourself as a child. Feel yourself in the moment as both the you of today *and* as the you of your childhood. Experience how good it feels to love yourself!

Visualization: See whichever part of you that you believe needs help represented by a child version of you. For example, you might feel a lack of self-worth. See yourself as a shy two-year-old or an insecure seven-year-old. Give the younger you a hug and tell him or her that everything is going to be okay—that you are going to figure it out. Tell the younger you not to take life so seriously and to do more of what you enjoy. Tell the younger you, "I love you." Say that "Life is a work in progress, and we all want to get to the top of the mountain, but all the happiness and growth occurs while we are climbing it." Say whatever else comes to you in the moment that the child might need to hear. Have compassion for yourself, and feel the love that comes naturally when you connect with your heart energy.

Stepping into Masculine Energy

Give yourself a pep talk and do something. Do anything! Remember that masculine energy is all about action. For you to step into your masculine energy, you need to feel the passion, strength, and drive that will propel you forward in your life. To access your masculine energy, think about something you have been afraid to do.

Visualization: Pretend you are an elite athlete about to step onto the court for the championship game. Think about how you would be feeling before you leave the locker room. Think about the focus you would have. Think about the intensity of the moment and the exhilaration of finally getting to be in a moment you have been training for. Think about all the desires you have had to be the best, to be number one, to be a champion.

Now . . . become the coach. Tell yourself you are ready for this moment and you have been dreaming about this moment all your life. Look into your own eyes and say, "You got this. There is no better time than right now. Everything that you have done has prepared you for this moment. Go out there and become the powerful force you know you can be." Say whatever else comes to your mind that will help you build momentum so that you can take action.

Then, without delay, when you are feeling the inspiration, take some form of action. It might be calling someone to schedule an appointment. It might be asking someone out on a date. It might be getting on the treadmill and moving. Wherever your championship game takes place, get on the court! It is by doing just one thing that you will begin to build momentum and learn how to step into your masculine energy when you need it.

BE ABSOLUTELY YOU

The philosopher Martin Heidegger said, "A person is not a thing or process, but an opening through which the Absolute can manifest." We each embody this universal Law of Gender that explains how two seemingly different qualities are ultimately part of one universal whole. By embodying both ends of the masculine-feminine spectrum, each of us is an opening for light to flow and a gateway for the Absolute to manifest. As you go through life, through your MASTERY games of Hide & Seek, and you discover your truth, remember that you are the precious vehicle through which the Absolute . . . *You* . . . can manifest.

By embodying both ends of the masculine-feminine spectrum, each of us is an opening for light to flow and a gateway for the Absolute to manifest.

While it is your individual journey, everyone and everything is intimately connected, and your ability to have compassion in your thoughts and actions will only bring that same beautiful compassionate energy back to you. As you have gone through these chapters and participated in the Personal Rulebook Plays, you have started discovering your own truth. Your MASTERY games of Hide & Seek are about finding *You.* The truth of who you are is within each game and is just waiting for you to discover it. Have fun with the process! Know that you are here in this world to enjoy—to savor—the experience. Whether you get hung up on something that doesn't feel right, or you are in the zone and flying high, continue to look for *your* truth in any situation. Continue to honor who you are and what you want out of your life. Continue to find ways to connect with what is true for you. Continue to embrace the brilliant and ever-changing unique individual that only you can be.

PART THREE

FINDING THE BALANCE

ᴱENGAGE WITH ᴵINTEGRITY

*F*inding the Balance begins with the *E* in the MASTERY acronym: Engage with Integrity. To become a master of anything, you must be so in tune with your craft that you become one with it. There is a level of inspiration that only comes when you are completely in touch with the present moment, meaning you are in touch with your true Self, your surroundings, the task at hand, and others involved.

Life's path, as well as your MASTERY games of Hide & Seek, is filled with twists and turns that constantly leave you looking for your footing. Your goal is not to find a balance and intend to always stay there, but instead it is to constantly, and consistently, be looking for your center as you move through each day. Balance does not have to mean everything is equal. Let me repeat that . . . balance does *not* have to mean everything is equal. Finding the Balance in your MASTERY game of Hide & Seek is your opportunity to find your *own* version of balance, learn what that "center" feels like to you, and develop habits that will help you find your way back to that center when something throws you off.

Balance does not have to mean everything is equal.

One of the most common causes of feeling off-kilter is acting in a way that is not authentic. We are each unique individuals and there are millions of people who believe their way is the "right" way. All too often I coach someone who feels guilty because he isn't following the rules he's been taught. These rules can come from parents, religion, government, companies, or other peers. Now don't get me wrong, I'm not about to tell you to disregard all the rules and do your own thing. But in a way I am going to tell you to do just that (wink, wink)!

Rules are made up by people who have a reason for making the rule, which usually boils down to things like control, financial gain, safety, or harmony. If parents have a rule that bedtime is nine o'clock because their teenager needs sleep, then they are making that rule because they believe it is in the best interest of their child. If the police arrest you because you decide to break into someone else's house and take their things, your ensuing jail time is because they are enforcing rules designed for the safety and harmony of everyone in the country. Some rules definitely make sense, yet others seem to lack . . . *common* sense! I will refrain from examples here because most often when we find rules that just don't make sense to us, it is because we don't see the logic in the rule. I'm sure you can think of at least five things that you would call "ridiculous" rules if you took a few minutes. Rather than getting you all huffy about things you find foolish though, let's move into how the idea of rules helps you create a level of personal mastery in your life.

The idea within your MASTERY games of Hide & Seek is to uncover what your rules are, and then engage with integrity in all you say and do. *Integrity* is defined as the state of being whole and undivided. Engaging with integrity means that you are undivided—at one with yourself. Ever heard the saying, "I've got to be true to myself"? This phrase is simply saying, "I am committed to engaging with integrity." It means that you are living authentically—that everything you do and say is congruent with how you feel. Integrity is just another way to describe the alignment we talked about in Chapter 5: Achieve through Alignment.

For you, this may be one of the easiest concepts within the MAS-TERY game. Or it may be a far reach to feel comfortable letting down your guard and allowing others to see the real you. As we explore the different ways to engage with integrity in your MASTERY games of Hide & Seek, you will find that the answers are not always black and white. You will see that life is dynamic and so are the situations you find yourself in. Yet, before we can go into the specifics of how to engage with integrity, we need to explore the foundation that you must have in order to line up with your integrity. This foundation begins as a personal journey inward. It is a journey that leads to a deep knowing and love for yourself and brings you to a place of balance, which leads to self-esteem.

SELF-ESTEEM

Self-esteem is a vital attribute to living a life of balance and integrity. It is through self-esteem that we are able to thrive and grow more fully into all that we can become. Self-esteem in your MASTERY game of Hide & Seek is an outward symbol of balance and clarity. It is in this state of deep balance, harmony, and authenticity that you experience keen states of well-being and your inherent worthiness. You feel inspired. You are able to look at any situation with a wholehearted conviction that you will be okay, and you will do what is right for you.

True self-esteem is not one of ego or an inflated sense of one's self. Genuine self-esteem comes from your ability to confide in yourself by realigning with the inner *You*, moment to moment. And when that sense of self-worth is authentic, watch out! You will light up like a shooting star and bless the world around you. When you feel balanced on the inside, you are radiant on the outside. You attract recognition and validation, yet you do not feel arrogance or conceit. Genuine self-esteem is expressed in the world as a radiant confidence that is not above or below others but instead a steady, grounded center that you are able to depend on. It is a feeling of inherent confidence and trust.

*Genuine self-esteem comes from your ability to confide in
yourself by realigning with the inner You, moment to moment.*

When we express ourselves without effort, when we "don't hold
back," we know we are in balance; we're in alignment. This is our
indicator that we are going with the flow of life. But when we are out
of balance or in a state of confusion or chaos, we tend to close up, try
too hard, and doubt our abilities. Part three of your MASTERY
games—where you are Finding the Balance—is designed to help you
restore your balance and get back on your path when you find yourself off in the bushes.

TWO CAUSES = OUT OF BALANCE

Within the MASTERY games of Hide & Seek, there are two root causes
that throw us out of balance: overextending and overanalyzing. When
we overextend ourselves and don't set limits, we become depleted and
inactive. When we overanalyze situations, we create doubt, confusion,
and interference. Both of these can temporarily cause us to lose sight
of our center. *Temporary* is a relative term though, isn't it? It may be
counted in minutes, or days, or even years depending on where you
choose to put your focus as you are in a situation that is challenging
your sense of balance.

Overextending

Have you ever said yes, when you knew you should have said no?
Have you ever said, "I have such a hard time saying no"? These are
signs that you may be consistently choosing to overextend yourself
and consequently losing your balance. If you often find yourself
feeling exhausted or having a tough time feeling motivated to do

anything, you may have "overextending-itis." No, that is not a real word, but you get my drift. I know overextending-itis very well because it took me years (thirty-eight to be exact) to realize that my all-or-nothing habit of living was making my life a lot harder than it needed to be. I am now in a place of awareness about overextending where I am able to recognize what feels right to me, and I do my best to honor that grounded voice of stability within me. I still find myself overextended at times, but it is a far cry from the constant fatigue and shutdown that was common in my life before.

Setting limits is a skill that many people find difficult to master. I say it is a skill because it takes practice for most of us to even know exactly what our limits are to begin with. Whether you are setting limits with your children, creating perimeters with coworkers, or discovering personal boundaries in any area of your life, it takes practice to know where to draw the lines. You may even be like me where I just had so much I wanted to accomplish that I had trouble drawing the lines for myself. I thought I could fit everything in because I wanted to be able to do it all.

Question: Is it called "practice" because you want to get it right all the time? Of course not. Practice means that sometimes you get it right and sometimes you don't. Being able to push your limits is a natural part of being alive—just like lifting weights stresses a muscle, which in turn repairs itself and builds more muscle. You learn how it feels to be off balance when you're pushing your limits. And by knowing how it feels to be out of whack, it gives you the ability to also know what it feels like to be grounded and centered.

Without boundaries and the ability to say no, you can feel completely trampled. Even when you bring it on yourself, you still end up feeling drained and unmotivated. In fact, oftentimes—most of the time—overexertion is brought on by yourself. This could be considered a discouraging insight, or it could be another game of Hide & Seek where you are learning to reach for a new level of personal mastery. Look at your fatigue or depression as a sign that you need to look for the *You* that is hiding somewhere deep within. Finding *You* will bring you a sense of hope if you are feeling down. Finding *You* will bring you vitality when you are tired. Over time, as you practice finding the balanced place within you, you'll become a champion at setting boundaries and not overcommitting.

Personal Rulebook Play
OVEREXTENDING

Get out your Personal Rulebook. Write down at least one area of your life where you are struggling with overextending-itis. For example, it could be that you always say yes, even when you want to say no. Then answer the following questions:

✦ What are the consequences of overextending yourself?

✦ How does your body respond?

✦ How do you respond mentally and emotionally?

✦ How do you cope with feeling exhausted or down in the dumps?

We will come back to this Personal Rulebook Play at the end of this chapter once you've learned the various tools for helping you engage with integrity. For now, this is your chance to see your starting points so you can think about where you want to be when you cross the finish line.

Overanalyzing

Overanalyzing-itis is also a "disease" I know very well. When we overthink things, we also make life a lot harder than it needs to be. How often have you spent countless hours—or days—thinking about something only to end up being more confused about it than when you started? This is because when we ponder a question from every angle possible, we see problems from every angle. And as we see problems from every angle, we start to feel overwhelmed and wonder whether we can ever figure out an answer. All of this interference that we are creating through our thoughts moves our attention away from our center and . . . off the path we go again, right into the bushes! Does this sound familiar?

Our minds are powerful machines that can be a blessing or a curse, depending on how we choose to focus. Your choice of focus has the power to bring you answers, as well as the power to bring you more questions. "More questions?" you ask. Yes, indeed, more questions. How often have you started asking questions about something and you found another question before you answered the first one?

> *Your choice of focus has the power to bring you answers, as well as the power to bring you more questions.*

For instance, a gal asks a friend where she wants to have lunch. The friend responds by asking, "What are you in the mood for?" The first gal starts pondering what kind of food sounds good and answers by asking her friend another question, "What sounds good to you?" The friend says she doesn't care and starts naming restaurants that are nearby. It takes ten minutes just to figure out where they want to eat. Multiply this by the "overwhelm factor" when you have six people joining the conversation! Have you ever been in a situation like this and felt frustrated, wanting to say, "Can we just make a decision already? I'm starving!"?

This may be a lighthearted example of how overanalyzing can play out to create more interference and cause confusion, but it shows how easy we can be thrown off balance. On the other hand, if you were part of this conversation and you were really connected to your center, while the confusion and questions are being thrown around, you would likely be entertained by the hilarity of the situation and just enjoy watching everyone debate about where to go. From your place of groundedness, you might even throw in a suggestion that you think will help the group be more decisive. Once the decision is made, you would gladly head off with your friends to enjoy lunch.

I have to giggle thinking about this example because it is often the case where women will find themselves in a situation like this. Why? Because women operate primarily from their heart, so they are concerned about others' feelings. They want to make sure that everyone feels good and that everyone is "happy." Men, on the other hand, operate primarily from their head. They aren't thinking about feelings; they are simply thinking about the answer to the question! So, this same conversation between two guys would go something like this: One guy asks his friend where he wants to have lunch, and his friend says, "Let's go to the steakhouse." He says, "Okay," and they head off to the steakhouse for lunch. It takes about ten seconds rather than ten minutes to figure out where they are going to eat.

Knowing what we know about masculine and feminine from Chapter 7: Think with Compassion, this raises a good question. If it is our minds that we are using to overanalyze, how is it that the masculine version of the above scenario could make the decision much easier and quicker than the feminine version? Isn't the masculine operating from the head? The answer is yes, but that leads us to another question. The head is where we house our brain, but where is our mind?

It would seem that the equation for an overanalyzing mind doesn't just involve the brain, but also involves the intuitive heart. And maybe, just maybe, when the brain and the heart are out of balance, you feel doubt, confusion, and interference. But once they align, you find clarity.

Now, we go back to the example above where the guys make the decision about lunch more easily than their female counterparts. Does that mean that men are more in balance than women? As my husband will say, "Guys are simple. We are not that complicated. When someone asks us a question, we don't think about anything else, we just answer the question."

Does it make you wonder? Maybe being a little less complicated is an easier way to live! It has certainly crossed my mind. Yet, the complications in life are what challenge us to find our balance. So is complication really all that bad? Maybe not so much. In fact, if women are the complicated ones, why is it that men are so attracted to them? (Okay, I'll stop overanalyzing. Ha ha!)

Personal Rulebook Play
OVERANALYZING

Get out your Personal Rulebook, and think about areas in your life where you tend to overanalyze. Write down an example of something you are currently stuck on or something from the past that was difficult for you to find clarity around. Think about why you feel or felt doubt or confusion about this issue. Then, answer the following questions:

+ Are you concerned about what others will think if you make one decision over another?

+ Are you not sure that you have enough information about how the decision is going to impact your life?

+ Are you concerned that you're going to make the wrong choice and regret it later?

+ What are other reasons or questions that are creating interference for you?

Just as with the previous Personal Rulebook Play, we will come back to this Play at the end of the chapter and rethink where you want to cross the finish line to this play.

TWO SOLUTIONS = RESTORATION OF BALANCE

While there are two root causes that throw us out of balance in the MASTERY game of Hide & Seek, there are also two solutions that help us restore balance: prudence and swiftness. *Prudence* is defined as the quality of acting with concern, or showing care and thought, for the future. Within your Hide & Seek games, it refers to having the wisdom to act from a centered place. When referring to a person, *centered* is defined as well balanced and confident or serene. We have already touched on this in the previous discussions—finding that centered place within you will help you find your own balance and engage with integrity.

Swiftness, as it relates to restoring balance, means having the willingness to stop procrastinating and take immediate action with direct communication. Both of these solutions allow us to step out of the inertia, confusion, and frustration that come with imbalance. Knowing how to recognize which solution you need is the basis of these Hide & Seek games. When exploring how to engage with integrity, you must ask yourself, *What do I need here? Do I need to be more grounded? Do I need to take action? Do I need to communicate how I'm feeling more clearly?*

Prudence

As I have mentioned many times already, being centered is crucial to having clarity. Clarity leads to integrity. Integrity leads to a fun and fulfilling life. Prudence means that you take action when you are balanced and centered. As a kid, did you ever spin around in circles until you were so dizzy that you had trouble standing up? I remember doing it when I was a kid, and it always makes me smile when my four-year-old does it today. In fact, I remember playing with my friends as a child, spinning around, and then trying to run in our yard. We would crack up laughing as we watched each other take about three to six steps before crashing onto the grass. This same concept applies as you use prudence to master engaging with integrity. If you are trying to start running when your thoughts have been "spinning around," or you don't have solid footing, you're going to come crashing down. While it was funny when we were kids, it doesn't always feel so fun as adults.

What does that center feel like for you? This is one goal of your MASTERY games. Start to think about what "balanced" looks and feels like to you. What are some words that would describe your perception of being balanced? For some, being balanced might be having a comfortable mix of obligations and free time. For others, it might be staying very active but always getting enjoyment from the activities. Still yet, others might need ample downtime to restore and rejuvenate. Being balanced can be defined in as many ways as there are people on the planet. The question is: How do you define it in your life?

How do you tap into that wisdom that guides you toward action or inactivity? If you've been doing your Personal Rulebook Plays as you've been reading *Hide & Seek*, you have already been developing and discovering ways to tap into this wisdom. Remember in Chapter 4: Maximize Your Impact, we talked about trusting your gut? Your gut is the wisdom, the little voice whispering in your ear, telling you which way is right for you. Or how about in Chapter 7: Think with Compassion, when you learned that connecting to your feminine energy—your heart—allows you to access your inner wisdom? These are skills that help you to be prudent. They help you know what feels right and how or when to take action.

Personal Rulebook Play
WHAT BALANCE MEANS TO ME

Grab your Personal Rulebook, and think about what balance means to you in your life. Then, respond to the following questions:

✦ How do you define balance?

✦ What does being centered feel like to you?

✦ Think about a time when you were in a situation where things just didn't feel right to you. What did you do? How did it turn out? How did you feel as you were going through it?

✦ Think about a time when things just felt good. Everything about the situation seemed to be pointing to *yes*. What did you do in that situation? How did it turn out? How did you feel as you were going through it?

✦ What could you do to help remind yourself to use prudence—being in a centered place—when you are making decisions, such as the decision to say no when you don't want to overextend yourself?

Swiftness

The second solution to restoring balance is swiftness. *Swift* is defined as moving or being capable of moving at high speeds. When you incorporate swiftness into your MASTERY games of Hide & Seek, it allows you to step out of the confusion and take action. In fact, by definition, *swift* means being capable of moving at high speeds. When you have clarity, decisions are easy. Answers come quickly. You are able to move at quick speeds because you are up to speed with your true Self.

I remember starting my business as a financial advisor. I had no clients and was new in town. I had to rely on my persistence and perseverance to go back to prospects and hear "no thanks," time and time again, before I would finally hear a "Yes, let's do business together." (Cue the angels singing! *Ahhhhhhhhh!*) I had to learn to play games with myself to help me keep moving when I just didn't feel like picking up the phone and making another call. I remember thinking, *I know it takes seven no's to get to a yes. I've contacted this person five times. Only two more to go.* I would make deals with myself like, *Make ten more calls and then you can go over to Starbucks and get a mocha.* I would find anything that would motivate me to pick up the phone to call someone or go out and meet people face-to-face.

One technique that worked really well for me and that I later taught others as they were building their businesses was to be swift. Just pick up the phone and start dialing. Don't think about all of the scenarios that could play out if the person picks up on the other end of the phone. Don't check your teeth in the mirror, call home to check in, or go through your to-dos to see if your assistant has added anything new. Just pick up the phone and dial! It was a way to keep inertia from setting in. It allowed me to build momentum and get in the zone.

What I found most amazing was that there was one thing—ONE THING—that worked best when I was in a funk. One thing that worked when things had slowed to the point of almost no movement and I was feeling out of sync, hesitant, timid, and anxious. The one thing that would get things moving again—quickly, most of the time—was to get out of the box. What that meant to me was to step out of my comfort zone and do something, anything, that I knew would be beneficial to my business and me. Almost every time I would get a surge of energy and motivation because it either worked out fantastically, or I felt really proud of myself for trying.

Other times, I would do something that would make me feel really good. For example, I would call a client who always loved hearing from me. Someone who I knew would be happy to hear my voice on the other end of the phone. It was simply a feel-good call that would start to relieve the hesitation or anxiety I was feeling. Then as soon as

I hung up with that client I would pick up the phone and make a call I had previously been dreading. A funny thing would happen. The certainty and happiness in my voice would oftentimes impact the conversation in a very positive way. When it didn't, I was riding the wave of positive momentum and was able to let it go and pick up the phone again. If you can find something you enjoy doing that makes you feel better when you are feeling stuck, it will go a long way toward helping you get on your surfboard and ride the positive momentum wave.

Swiftness to restore balance and bring you back to your center means getting out of the comfort box you may be trapped in. It doesn't have to be something dramatic, although it could be, but it does have to be some immediate form of action in the direction you want to move toward. It's your willingness to drop procrastination and take immediate action that will restore your balance. It's your ability to communicate clearly and candidly about what you want that will create a life full of integrity.

> *It's your willingness to drop procrastination and take immediate action that will restore your balance.*

Personal Rulebook Play
GETTING THINGS MOVING AGAIN

Get out your Personal Rulebook, and think about any areas of your life where you get stuck and struggle to get things moving again. Then, answer the following questions:

◆ What are the areas you just identified and why do you think you get stuck there?

◆ What ways can you see how overextending or overanalyzing might play a role in your struggle?

+ What are some ways you could use swiftness to help get things moving again? For example: What are at least three specific actions you could take that would force you to step out of your comfort zone? Who could you ask to support you, to be an accountability partner, who would help you follow through with your commitment to yourself? Is there something you love to do that leaves you feeling energized?

Take Action and Engage with Integrity:

+ Do one of the three specific things you identified above immediately.

+ Call your support person and tell her or him what you want to do, and ask her or him to help you.

+ Do something you love, and once you are feeling energized, without thinking about it, do one of your three specific things!

TOOLS FOR RESTORING BALANCE

To manifest all that you truly are, you must find tools to help you find your center and engage in your life with integrity. There are no magic tools that will help everyone, but instead it is a process of learning what helps you find your center. Meditation is one technique that many people believe helps them stop the noise in their head and reconnect with their body and inner Self. Others find that joyful sense of connectedness when they are doing some activity that they enjoy— exercise, for instance, or gathering with like-minded people or playing with a dog. There really are countless tools people can use to find their balance. For your MASTERY games of Hide & Seek, I would like to offer four concepts that can help you develop an understanding of how to approach situations as they come up in your life. These are the Confusion-Clarity Continuum, the Focus Continuum, the Momentum and Timing Advantage, and Habits and Rituals Awareness. We'll spend the remainder of this chapter looking at each of these tools for restoring your balance.

The Confusion-Clarity Continuum

Everything in the universe is constantly moving, and the situations of your life are ever changing. The key is realizing that there is a constant flow to life, and as my mother has often said, "This, too, shall pass." Going with the flow is the easiest way to get what you want. It's like floating down a river. If you decide to go tubing, do you end up downstream or upstream? Downstream, of course. They don't call it a lazy river for nothing. Yet, *lazy* would not be the word I would use to describe going with the natural flow of life. Smart, easy, or enjoyable, maybe, but not lazy. In fact, it takes work to stay focused on the things that are most important to you. Just like it takes work to get the tubes ready, the snacks packed, and the vehicles to the drop-off and pick-up points at the river, it takes work to know what you value most, where your boundaries are, and how you want to engage with the world. Bottom line: Lazy leaves you confused. Focus leaves you clear-minded.

Getting back to that lazy river idea: Why do they call it a lazy river? Because once you get in your tube, it is a gentle and relaxing ride. You don't have to paddle. You don't have to kick. Most people don't even get out to go to the bathroom! (Come on, you know you've done it.) You did most of the work prior to getting in your tube. Floating down the river is your reward.

It's the same thing in life. When you do the work to gain clarity about what you want in life, your reward is getting to enjoy the flow that comes with that clarity. And just as we learned when we explored the Law of Rhythm, the pendulum will always be swinging back and forth. One direction may feel like flowing down the lazy river, while the other may feel like running into a hundred-mile-per-hour wind. The lazy river comes from clarity. The hurricane comes from confusion.

> *The lazy river comes from clarity.*
> *The hurricane comes from confusion.*

But does this mean that your goal should be to never have confusion? Confusion is what leads to clarity. In your MASTERY games, your greatest challenges will come from delusion, illusion, and self-deception. Ever told yourself you can't do something because . . . (fill in the blank here)? Most of us are masters at coming up with excuses as to why things aren't working out for us. We create illusions about something before we have all the facts. We make up reasons for why we won't succeed even when we haven't given it a sincere chance. Clarity does not come from excuses. It comes from confusion.

When you are willing to challenge the veils of delusion, illusion, and self-deception, you will find your way to your center. This goes back to the self-esteem that we learned about earlier. When you can confide and trust in yourself, you lift the veil and see clearly. You develop self-love, self-trust, and self-respect. You also begin to get glimpses of the solutions to your problems.

You do this by understanding that just as the Law of Rhythm states, there is a constant movement from one end to another. For your Engage with Integrity MASTERY games, confusion and clarity are a never-ending continuum.

You are moving along the continuum at different paces and learn-

Confusion　　　　　　　　　Clarity

ing from each side as you progress. If you get overwhelmed, you might be moving at a snail's pace on the confusion side, but eventually, you will work through your confusion and glide into the clarity side. What a fun feeling to know that it is just a process, right? There's nothing wrong with you. You don't lack some ability to live the life you want. You are just playing on the Confusion-Clarity Continuum as you figure out what you value most and how you want to act, react, or engage.

To move out of confusion, it is necessary to have a shift in your mental outlook. Words that can help you see the kind of shift we're going for here are *opportunity, breakthrough, prosperity, abundance,* and *expansion.* When you are confused, it is easy to feel closed off, with a sense of heaviness and negativity. To shift yourself away from that end of the pendulum and turn yourself toward a more positive and expansive viewpoint, try the following:

- ❖ Be objective.
- ❖ Be flexible.
- ❖ Reach for new opportunities.
- ❖ Look for ways to be creative.

Expansion, abundance, and clarity come when you are willing to change and keep things moving by taking risks and being open to new opportunities. A risk might be asking someone out on a date or telling your partner that you feel really hurt when he or she makes you the brunt of jokes. It also might be jumping off the high diving board for the first time. Risks are simply those situations that get you out of your comfort zone and into taking action. And they often lead to "aha" moments when you awaken to possibilities that turn you toward more positive and expansive directions.

Be flexible, be objective, and be open-minded. When you are actively open to turning your life toward fortunate and positive outcomes, you find your way to the clarity side of the continuum, and naturally begin engaging with integrity in all you do.

Personal Rulebook Play
MY PLACE ON THE
CONFUSION-CLARITY CONTINUUM

Get out your Personal Rulebook and think about on which side of the confusion-clarity continuum you spend most of your time. Then, draw the Confusion-Clarity Continuum as shown on page 177. Think about where you are in your life right now and draw an X in the place where you see yourself at the moment. Then respond to the following:

✦ On a scale of 1–100 mph, write down how fast you are moving at the moment. Are you stuck in confusion, going 1 mph? Or maybe you are in confusion, but you are moving at a comfortable 35 mph? Or are you moving into clarity at 75 mph?

✦ Write down how you feel in the place you are right now. What words would you give to your emotions? *Frustrated? Depressed? Restless? Grateful? Excited?*

✦ Think about what you want to do with your X. Do you want to move it faster along the continuum to another point? Or do you want to slow it down a bit and savor the place you are in at the moment?

There are no right or wrong answers in this Play. This is a continuum. No matter where you are right now, you are going to be on the other side in the near future. Neither side is wrong; both sides bring you to your center. Did you notice that? On the continuum, the two hemispheres meet in the middle. That middle is just like your center. And just as we discussed earlier, balance doesn't mean both sides have to be equal. You can spend more time in clarity if you choose.

The Focus Continuum

Throughout this chapter I have mentioned focus about a gazillion times. So let's spend a little "focused time" discussing the dynamics of focus. And since we are using the visual aid of continuums, let's apply that same idea to focus. This continuum is made up of defocus, refocus, and laser-like focus.

No need to go through the way the continuum works. You know it never stops. You know it doesn't need to be balanced. You know you find your center where the two sides meet. What you are *about* to know is how to manage your focus. Remember when we talked about the river and learned that flowing down the river is the easy part, but most of the work happens prior to getting to the river? Then we talked about how focus takes work. It takes work to remain focused on what you find important. There are, literally, millions of distractions vying for your attention in today's world. The easy road, or river in this case, is to let your attention drift to whatever crosses your path. The work is discovering what you want to value most and then consciously choosing to put your attention there.

When you get stuck focusing on something that does not represent one of your core values, take a step back. Allow yourself to defocus your attention from that issue and think about something else: Something else that makes you feel good, like how yummy a strawberry tastes. Something else that you are passionate about, like a form of art, food, exercising, or your kids. Something else that you have to

Defocus

Refocus

Laser-Like
Focus

do, like finish a project at work. It doesn't really matter what you choose to help distract you so you can defocus on the hang-up. What does matter is that whatever you choose allows you to step away and get out of the negative emotional feeling you're experiencing.

Once you are able to get out of the negative emotion by defocusing your attention from the subject, you are able to refocus your attention on what matters most to you. Think about what your core values are and remind yourself of all the reasons those things matter to you. Think about how your life is better because those things matter to you. Think about how you can refocus your energy onto something that energizes you and fills you up with joy and satisfaction. All of these patterns of thought will help you find your balance.

Soon you will start to feel the positive emotions that come because you are now balanced and grounded in your center. At this point, begin to really zero in on what it is that you specifically love about your core values. If one of your values is the enjoyment of healthy food, think about the kinds of food you like. Think about the best meal you've ever had. Think about how eating healthily fuels your body and gives you energy and vitality to do all the other things you love to do. Really zero in on everything you love until you have developed a laser-like focus on what makes you happy. Just as a laser is able to burn through metal because of the intensity of the focused energy, you, too, can create an energy that is laser-like with your attention to the details.

Ever wanted something so much that you could vividly imagine it in your mind? You could hear it, see it, touch it, and taste it. More important, you could feel what it would be like to get it. This is an example of laser-like focus. I have watched countless examples of people who have been able to manifest anything they wanted through this process of the Focus Continuum. The skill of managing your focus is the most powerful skill you will learn through your MASTERY games. In fact, the principle of focus was the number-one boundary in the rules of the MASTERY game of Hide & Seek. And by now, you realize this skill is completely in your control, and you get to choose where you put your attention. The outcome: amazing results.

The skill of managing your focus is the most powerful skill you will learn through your MASTERY games.

Personal Rulebook Play
MY CORE-VALUES LIST

Grab your Personal Rulebook. In this Play, you will be creating a list of your core values. If you aren't really clear about what they are, brainstorming is a great way to begin identifying them. Do the following:

Write down all of the things you value most. Whatever it is for you—include everything you can identify: From character, achievements, compassion, and integrity to family, friends, and self-love. From animals, food, and exercise to cars, shopping, and working. From the deepest desires in your heart to the people in your life and the physical objects that bring you joy. This is your list and only you know what you value and what helps you find your balance.

Now that you have a working list of your core values, respond to the following questions in your Personal Rulebook and practice the activities:

✦ If you had to narrow your list down to five words that would be the foundation of all your core values, what would those top five be?

✦ Take these top five values and put them somewhere you will be sure to see them every day. For example, make these values the scrolling screen saver on your computer. Or frame pictures that represent them and put them around your house or office. Or write them in your journal or rulebook each day and include something that happened that day that represented one or more of those five values.

♦ As you go through your week, look for opportunities to practice your focusing skills. When you find yourself thinking, *I don't like this*, pull your focus away (defocus), put your attention on one of your core values (refocus), and once you start feeling the positive shift in your emotions, get laser-like with specifics on how you can incorporate that core value into your experience.

The Momentum and Timing Advantage

The next concept that can help you develop an understanding of how to approach situations as they come up in your MASTERY games of Hide & Seek is knowing how to use timing and momentum to your advantage. These two factors are present in everything you experience. If you meet the love of your life on a trip to the coffee shop, win the state championship in your sport, or trip on a raised sidewalk and break your leg, momentum and timing were involved.

You have control over momentum and timing through your focus and alignment. In Chapter 5: Achieve through Alignment, we talked about how the Law of Attraction will bring to you whatever you focus on. Momentum and timing are part of the equation that allows for you to manifest anything in your life. Because everything is always in motion, there is a speed of momentum that is always present. Just like you could be going 1–100 mph on your Confusion-Clarity Continuum, your speed of momentum is a factor in every situation.

How do you use that momentum to your advantage? You learn how to adjust the speed. And we just explored how to adjust the rate of your momentum in the Focus Continuum. If things are moving too fast for you, draw your attention away (defocus) and as you do, the momentum toward that subject or situation will slow down. Remember, "Where your focus goes, your energy flows." As you then put your attention on something else (refocus), you can begin to change the direction of your momentum. Then, once you are headed in the right direction (you are aligned with your true Self and core values), you can start speeding up the momentum by getting laser-like with your focus. This is how you control momentum with your focus and alignment.

Timing, on the other hand, may seem a little more difficult to control. If you are thinking about control in the typical sense of the word, where you are trying to make things happen by taking action, then it is absolutely out of your control most of the time. Timing, as it relates to your ability to create in your life, is dependent upon your ability to find *You* in your MASTERY games of Hide & Seek. When you are aligned with *You,* your timing becomes impeccable. It is not because you are trying to make things happen, but instead you are inspired to take action or remain still. It is through this inspiration that comes from your inner Self that you are able to control timing. Timing is simply having all the pieces of the puzzle come together. And when you are balanced and connected to your center, your *You,* then there is a greater Intelligence that is working with you to put together the pieces of the puzzle.

When you are aligned with **You,**
your timing becomes impeccable.

When you are willing to give up the idea that you have to work really hard to make things happen, you will find that things happen effortlessly and in perfect timing for you. The only work you need to do is prepare for the lazy-river ride. Remain focused on what is important to you and find your center. The rest will work itself out because the current in the river knows intuitively how to get you downstream.

Personal Rulebook Play
EXPERIMENTING WITH TIMING AND MOMENTUM

Get out your Personal Rulebook. This Play will be an experiment in timing and momentum. Write down your intention to try this experiment for the next month: Pull your attention away from trying to *make* things happen in your life, and put your attention on the following:

✦ Clarity: Get clear about what you want in your life. Be very specific about the details with laser-like focus. Do whatever you need to do to *feel* it as if you already have it in your life.

✦ Balance: Get aligned with your inner Self, find your center, make decisions, and take action from that center; engage with integrity.

That's all you have to do! Just keep turning your attention to clarity and balance. When you feel clear-minded and grounded, you will be amazed at how timing and momentum magically start working in your favor. Jot down any observations you make over the course of the month under this Play.

Habits and Rituals Awareness

The last concept of Engage with Integrity is creating awareness of, and purposefully developing, habits and rituals. Habits are behaviors that you do over and over again. Rituals are purposeful actions. Most of our hang-ups come from patterns of bad habits. Within your MASTERY games, you have the opportunity to expose, redesign, or replace habits that are not serving you. We each have patterns of doing or saying things that make our life harder than it needs to be. However, these habits don't have to be treated like skeletons in your closet. If you choose to accept the habit for what it is, simply an action that you continue to do over and over again, you can release the guilt, judgment, and resistance you have toward it.

Once you release the tension you feel about a bad habit, it becomes exponentially easier to release the habit itself. This happens because you begin to defocus on the "problem." As you do that, you become more balanced and you begin to open up to possibilities of new habits that better serve you. Have you ever struggled with something for years and finally you were able to shift yourself away from it for good? I bet if you look back at the shift, you will find that you, in some way, released your resistance to it. And in that releasing, you most likely developed another habit, or ritual, that served you in a better way.

Once you release the tension you feel about a bad habit, it becomes exponentially easier to release the habit itself.

Sometimes people will go from one bad habit to another. A common example is quitting smoking but turning to food to replace the habit of physically bringing your hand to your mouth, emotionally filling a void, or mentally needing something to do. When you engage with integrity, you consciously make choices that serve you and are in your best interest. This means replacing a bad habit with a good habit. And one of the easiest ways to do that is to use rituals.

Ritual is defined as a series of actions or a type of behavior regularly and invariably followed by someone. Rituals are purposeful actions. They can promote bad habits or good habits. Choosing to get up in the morning and put on your running shoes to work out is a ritual. Choosing to light up a cigarette and drink a soda is a ritual. One is promoting your health and the other is degrading it.

You always have a choice as to which rituals you want to adopt in your life, and you can be purposeful in your choices so that they regularly uplift you. I used to drink a mocha filled with sugar and caffeine every morning. Now I love making fresh hazelnut milk and putting a shot of decaf espresso and vanilla extract in it. Choosing to find a healthier alternative to my ritual of enjoying my morning drink was a way to turn an unhealthy habit into a healthier one. I still get unbelievable enjoyment out of it. In fact, I savor the taste of my freshly made hazelnut milk with a touch of espresso and a hint of vanilla. It tastes far better and is ten times more satisfying to me than my old mocha.

Personal Rulebook Play
BAD HABITS I'D LIKE TO CHANGE

Get out your Personal Rulebook, and write down one to three behaviors that have become "bad" habits for you that you would like to change. Spend a few minutes thinking about what you like about these habits and what you dislike about them. Then respond to the following questions:

What kind of rituals have you developed that reinforce the habit(s)?

✦ What would you gain by choosing to release this pattern of behavior?

✦ What new ritual(s) can you start incorporating into your life to shift your momentum away from the habit that is not serving you and toward a habit that is supporting you?

For the next thirty days, make a commitment to start incorporating the new rituals you identified above into, and releasing the old rituals from, your life. Remember to be gentle with yourself. Releasing the tension, self-judgment, or guilt makes it exponentially easier to make shifts in your life.

CULTIVATE THE HABIT OF MASTERY

Mastery comes through practice so be grateful for the opportunities you have to practice not overextending or overanalyzing. You find your balance every time you go through an experience that challenges you. And it is an intoxicating feeling when you find your way back to your center and feel the inherent confidence and trust that comes to you once you are there.

The Engage with Integrity part of your MASTERY games of Hide & Seek is your practice to help you find your own balance. Use the tools and clarity you have discovered during this chapter to change the way you approach your life. Trust that you have everything at your disposal to create whatever you desire. You will find that as you live in a more balanced state and make conscious choices from that vantage point, your life will unfold into a beautiful masterpiece that is far greater than you ever imagined.

Personal Rulebook Playback: OVEREXTENDING

Grab your Personal Rulebook and look back at the Personal Rulebook Play: Overextending, which you did earlier in this chapter. Now that you've learned the tools to help you engage with integrity, respond to the following from your new vantage point:

✦ You know your starting points. You wrote down answers to the following questions for an area of your life where you struggle with overextending-itis.

✦ In your rulebook, write in your own areas such as "always saying yes," "not setting limits," or "taking reckless actions." Then answer the questions below to understand how each of those behaviors affects you.

✦ What are the consequences that you deal with when you overextend yourself? For example, ask yourself, "What are the consequences when I always say yes?"

✦ How does your body respond? For example, ask yourself, "How does my body respond when I'm always saying yes to others? Do I get wiped out?"

✦ How do you respond mentally and emotionally? For example, ask yourself, "How does it make me feel about myself when I say yes, when I really want to say no? Inauthentic? Disappointed in myself?"

✦ How do you cope with feeling exhausted or down in the dumps? For example, ask yourself, "What do I do to make myself feel better or console myself? Overeat? Become depressed? Lash out at others?"

✦ Repeat this process for every area you have recognized that causes you to overextend yourself.

✦ Next think about how you could use your Engage with Integrity tools that you've just learned to start changing the way you engage in your life—for example, going from "always saying yes" to "wisely committing," from "not setting limits" to "setting healthy boundaries," or from "taking reckless actions" to "being prudent with my actions."

✦ Write down what you want to experience by not overextending yourself. Be specific about the details of how you want to feel, physically and mentally.

✦ Once you can imagine what it will feel like to not be overextended, practice staying balanced by knowing where you are on your Confusion-Clarity Continuum.

✦ Use your Focus Continuum to bring you back to your center as you go through your day. Remember, there will be countless distractions vying for your attention. It's normal and it's necessary so you can experience the fullness of your life. You get to choose where you put your attention. Your goal is to align those choices with your core values.

Personal Rulebook Playback
OVERANALYZING

Grab your Personal Rulebook and look back at the Personal Rulebook Play: Overanalyzing, which you did earlier in this chapter. In that Play, you wrote down an example of something you are currently stuck on or something from the past that was difficult for you to find clarity around by answering the following questions:

✦ Are you concerned about what others will think if you make one decision over another?

✦ Are you not sure that you have enough information about how the decision is going to impact your life?

✦ Are you concerned that you're going to make the wrong choice and regret it later?

✦ What are other reasons or questions that are creating interference for you?

Rethink a new outcome for your life by following the same process above for this Rulebook Play.

✦ Write down what you want to experience by not overanalyzing. Be specific about the details of how you want to feel, physically and mentally.

✦ Once you can imagine what it will feel like to not overanalyze this situation, practice staying balanced by knowing where you are on your Confusion-Clarity Continuum.

✦ Use your Focus Continuum to bring you back to your center every time you begin to start analyzing the situation. Ask yourself, *Am I overanalyzing?* If you are asking lots of questions, the answer to this question is, "Yes!"

✦ If overanalyzing is a habit for you, at first, you will likely want to continue to think about the situation. If this is the case, your goal is to defocus and refocus your attention on the core values that will help you stay balanced. When you continue to put your attention on your core values, your answers for the situation will come to you effortlessly because your attention is on staying centered rather than trying to mentally figure it out.

CHAPTER NINE

RETREAT FOR SANITY

*H*ave you ever felt like you just wanted to crawl into a hole and get away from everything? This desire comes from not feeling nurtured. It is an indication that you need to take care of yourself, and it is the second part of Finding Your Balance. Retreat for Sanity is the R of *MASTERY*. This is one of my favorite parts of self-mastery because it feels *so* good! When you were young and in the peak of your childhood, taking time for yourself was likely how you spent the majority of your days!

What happened to change that childhood innocence and natural gravitation toward self-devotion? How did everything become so focused on the world we live in today, which is, for the most part, caught up in relentless cycles of "do more, be more, and have more"? While many people believe that being busy gives them a sense of self-worth, this style of living doesn't support the habit of self-care. And ironically, it is when you take care of yourself that you feel the worthiness that is inherently yours to begin with.

You will master Retreat for Sanity when you truly understand and incorporate the importance of nurturing yourself mentally, emotionally, spiritually, and physically. This holistic understanding of self-love is something we all need, and without it, you will feel disconnected from the *You* that is hiding in the MASTERY game of Hide & Seek. *You* loves everything about you and wants you to love you, too. Did you follow all those *yous?* Said a little differently, the God energy within you—your inner being—wants you to love yourself.

When I think about Retreat for Sanity, I envision a hammock under a palm tree on a beach with a warm breeze and the ocean waves lapping the shore. Doesn't that image just make you want to take a deep breath and slow down for a moment? To the same extent that finding your balance is important for you to engage in the world, it is essential to find your balance to gain sanity and inner peace.

MAKING THE SHIFT

Most of us don't grow into being adults with the belief that we should take care of ourselves first. Take care of others maybe, but taking care of yourself *before* you take care of others? Well, that's just "selfish." But in your MASTERY game of Hide & Seek, you don't win unless you put yourself first. For most, this is a huge shift in thought patterns that has to be accepted, but it is a shift worth considering because it allows you to creatively express yourself in unlimited and inspirational ways.

> *In your MASTERY game of Hide & Seek,*
> *you don't win unless you put yourself first.*

When you take time for yourself, you find your balance. You get grounded in your center. And as we have already learned in Chapter 8: Engage with Integrity, when you are centered, your life unfolds with ease. Remember, it's like drifting down a lazy river. The creative flow that accompanies this journey down the river is exhilarating. Nothing feels better than to be in sync with the flow of your life. Everything feels good: Your communication skills are sharp; ideas come to you with clarity; and you naturally want to follow what has heart and meaning for you. Internally and externally, you experience the unlimited possibilities of who you are. Every aspect of your being—mental, emotional, spiritual, and physical—is heightened, and you can't wait to see what's next.

Does any of this resonate with you? Are you able to see the difference in your life when you shift your mental outlook toward the mind-set of self-love? It gives you a sense of unlimited abundance and opportunity. If abundance and opportunity aren't good enough reasons to give this a shot, I don't know what is.

What does self-nurturance look like? It is like many other aspects of your MASTERY game of Hide & Seek. There are countless ways that self-nurturance can be yours. The only rule is that whatever avenue you choose, it fills you with a sense of peace and happiness. You might choose to take a bath, exercise, or eat something you love. Or you may go to the theatre, listen to music, buy a new shirt, or get a massage. See where I'm going with this? It doesn't matter what it is; it just matters that you get enjoyment and feel refreshed by doing it.

The preceding examples apply to the physical aspect of you, but you also have mental, emotional, and spiritual aspects to consider. What would mental self-nurturance look like for you? Positive affirmations, reading, or a stimulating conversation maybe? What would feed your emotional needs? You might hug someone you love, tell yourself that everything is going to work out, watch a "feel-good" movie. And finally, what could you do to spiritually nurture yourself? Maybe you'd meditate, listen to a sermon, take a walk in nature, or find a spiritual teacher. Are you beginning to grasp how easy it can be to find creative ways to love yourself? Simply do things that make you feel good.

Keep in mind that what works for you might not work for your friend or partner. Extroverts and introverts recharge differently. An introvert will recharge by being alone, and an extrovert recharges when he or she spends time with others. My husband and I are prime examples of this concept, so it was a profound awareness in my life when I first learned it.

When we first met, I was always trying to keep up with Chris, and in doing so, I was wearing myself out! When our then-therapist shared this idea of introverts and extroverts recharging in different ways, it was like she handed me a flashlight in my MASTERY game of Hide & Seek. All of a sudden it was so clear to me that it was okay for me to choose staying home to recharge (which is what I wanted to do!) rather than joining Chris to go snowboarding, meet up with friends, or whichever other social activity he was craving.

The other key "aha" moment for me in this introvert/extrovert recharging concept was that I was an introverted extrovert. That means that I am extroverted in many ways. I love being around other people, I am outgoing, and I enjoy sharing my energy with others. Yet, when it comes to how I recharge, find my center, and get grounded, I need time to be alone. This made *so* much sense to me because I love to be in my home. I love going home at the end of the day rather than going out for dinner or attending some event. I even prefer to work from home when I have the choice. These preferences all stem from my innate desire to Retreat for Sanity. It is the path I favor when it's time for me to recharge to stay balanced.

My husband is an extroverted extrovert. He gets stir crazy if he has to stay home all day. He has to get outside or, at the very least, tinker around the house with little projects. He loves being around other people, is outgoing, and enjoys sharing his energy with others, *and* he recharges by being active and engaging with others. I recharge by being solitary and being still. Accepting that we are different in how we approach this aspect of our lives—and allowing that difference to be okay—was a huge step in the personal and mutual happiness of our relationship.

Once you get into the mind-set that relishing the experiences of your life isn't selfish (it's the reason you are in the world), you will unlock the creative potential inside you and give more to the world than you could have ever given before. Doesn't that sound exciting? Doesn't it make you want to go out (or stay in!) and pamper yourself?

I bet you've experienced complete exhaustion at some point in your life. Since you know how that exhaustion feels, isn't it like a breath of fresh air to learn that in order to reach a level of personal mastery, you have to retreat for sanity at times?

So make the shift! Give yourself permission to stop denying your innate creative, expressive, and loving nature. Go back to your child-like innocence of believing you deserve to adore yourself and start doing things for yourself again. Make the world your playground. Feel the inspiration that comes when you look at your life with an expectation of fun, excitement, and a chance to explore, rather than filling it with the strain of obligations and requirements.

Personal Rulebook Play
WAYS TO SELF-NURTURE

Get out your Personal Rulebook. Make a list of all the things you can think of that would feel nurturing to you. Once you have brainstormed every possibility you can think of, categorize them into mental, emotional, spiritual, and physical. Be sure that you have an ample mix in all four areas. This holistic approach will help you develop a solid foundation of self-care.

Next, if retreating for sanity has not been one of your strong points, get out a calendar and assign an item from your list to every single day this month. It might be meditation in the morning or a bath before bed. The key to this Play is that you do a *minimum* of one thing every day that is just for you. Your goal is to start looking for ways to "retreat" throughout your day. These monumental shifts will refresh and recharge you all day long.

Over time, you'll want to do more and more for yourself because it will make you feel so good. Once you master the art of self-nurturing, you'll discover that rather than being "selfish," you end up giving more to those around you than you ever did before.

GRATITUDE HOLY GRAIL

Equal balance between self-nurturance and the nurturance of others is one sign of emotional integrity. Another sign is your ability to accurately express what you are feeling on the inside. When you master retreating for sanity, you are able to communicate your feelings from a place of trust rather than control, which comes from an open heart, a clear heart, and a trusting heart. This state of emotional integrity is the Holy Grail sitting within your emotional nature. You find the Holy Grail when you allow your true nature to lead you. Your true nature is love. It is a love that is constantly regenerating itself. It is a trusting love that is organically unfolding with no pushing or excessive exertion to make things happen. It is a love that goes through life with full abandon. There is no holding back, no resistance, and no need to protect itself.

> *You find the Holy Grail when you allow*
> *your true nature to lead you.*

This Holy Grail is a symbol of the emotional balance required to nurture, soothe, and restore yourself in equal proportion to how you nurture, soothe, and restore others. Some struggle with the term *equal* because it feels "unbalanced" for them to give the same amount of care to themselves when there are so many others with whom they need to split the other half. *Equal* in this MASTERY game is not defined in terms of measurement. It does not imply that you need to allot the same amount of time or the same amount of energy to yourself as you do to all of your loved ones combined. It is the intention that is placed on each side that counts. It's possible that the time and energy required to nurture, soothe, and restore yourself will be a fraction of the time and energy you spend doing the same for your family.

During a class I attended last year, I asked a small group of women, "Who has trouble with this concept of nurturing yourself?" Every single woman in the room raised her hand. I was shocked! For me, this concept is one of the gifts that I have been able to access and enjoy in this lifetime. I believe with all of my heart that I *must* take care of myself, and I see great benefits to myself and everyone else in my life because of it. Yet there are millions of people who are still searching for this Holy Grail that is right there waiting for them when they are ready to find it.

It's available to every one of us, and it is most easily found through gratitude. Through gratitude you are able to access the energy that is at the core of your emotional nature. This energy is the purest form of love. Gratitude for anything and everything will lead you to your Holy Grail. That includes gratitude for yourself—for all of the flaws you may see and for all of the gifts you may acknowledge. If you find yourself struggling with the insanity of life, begin thinking about all of the things you are grateful for. It will help you shift your awareness from the mental realm of chaos to the emotional realm of the unified heart. It is in your heart that you will find the all-encompassing, all-knowing, all-accepting . . . love.

Personal Rulebook Play
MY FEELINGS OF GRATITUDE

Get out your Personal Rulebook. In this Play, you will begin developing a practice of feeling gratitude every day. You may want to get a special journal that is just dedicated to capturing what you are grateful for each day, but use your rulebook for your first gratitude journal entry. Take the following steps:

✦ Begin each morning by writing down everything you can think of that you are grateful for—your bed, your body, your family, the sun, the moon, the stars, the trees, and so on. Spend five minutes making your gratitude list. Then sit quietly for at least five minutes and take in the feeling that comes from ruminating on all the items on your list.

✦ End by thanking your heart and God for the unconditional love that is waiting for you within your Holy Grail at any moment of the day. Set an intention to stay emotionally balanced so that you can live your day in union with that self-nurturing love.

Another option for incorporating this ritual of gratitude awareness doesn't even have to involve a journal. You can simply think about what you are grateful for all day long. Develop the habit of finding aspects to appreciate during your day, and you will constantly be relishing, retreating, and finding rejuvenation all day long.

LOVE WITH WISDOM—
BREAKING DESTRUCTIVE PATTERNS

Love with wisdom is the capacity to trust yourself without emotionally overextending or emotionally overprotecting yourself. It is the ability to give and receive love, as well as the internal energy that expresses love in the world. It is also the motivating energy that breaks down destructive patterns that hold you back from loving yourself and from showing love to others.

Through love with wisdom, you are able to transform undeveloped parts of yourself into awakened and passionate parts. This wisdom helps you see that through love, you are able to break destructive patterns that may be holding you back. In the MASTERY game of Hide & Seek, there are three resources that bring us love, and there is one hurdle that hinders our potential to feel—and give—love.

Through love with wisdom, you are able to transform undeveloped parts of yourself into awakened and passionate parts.

The hurdle is sorrow. When you are in a state of sorrow (unhappiness, despair, depression), you restrict your ability to feel or express love. This creates destructive patterns that lead to a vicious cycle of more misery. To break these patterns that are not serving you, there are three gifts that allow you to dissolve sorrow. They are:

1. Truth, coming from a place of integrity

2. Abundance, coming through emotional fulfillment

3. Focused intent, coming from a place of giving everything you can

For example, sorrow can be the result of not being true to who you are. You dissolve it through truth by communicating with honesty and integrity. Speaking your truth leads to a feeling of pride—or self-worth—because you are acknowledging your own belief that your opinion matters.

Sorrow can be the result of not clearly communicating your feelings. You can melt away that sorrow through abundance by expressing your feelings clearly and knowing that there is abundant love always flowing from your Holy Grail. Remember, your true nature is pure love and when you tap into it, it engulfs everything around you.

Finally, sorrow can come from uncertainty about your priorities and commitments. It dissipates through focused intent when you become clear about your priorities and where and with whom your commitments lie. As your intentions become more clear to you, it is easy to "give your all" to activities, projects, or people because passion evaporates any feelings of sorrow or sadness.

When you break destructive patterns through this profound wisdom that only comes through love, you will be able to contribute to the world with immense satisfaction. As you explore the Retreat for Sanity part of your MASTERY games of Hide & Seek, you will discover that you no longer want to restrict yourself with limiting or unproductive patterns. You will be able to transform your life. You will overcome sorrow from the past. You will prevent sadness in the future. And you will gain new perspectives on old issues and hang-ups.

When you are able to connect and merge with the profound love that is at the core of your being, you move beyond ego into trust and allowing. When you face old patterns and beliefs, and dissolve their power in your life, you discover the *You* within. You experience a universal love that not only heals your sorrows, but has the unlimited power to heal others as well.

Personal Rulebook Play
IDENTIFYING DESTRUCTIVE PATTERNS

Get out your Personal Rulebook. Write down any destructive patterns that are creating sorrow, sadness, depression, regret, or despair in your life. Then respond to the following:

✦ Is there a situation in your life in which you are not being true to yourself? What happened and how did you stray from your core values?

✦ Write down any problems you are experiencing—or unhappiness you are feeling—because you didn't communicate accurately.

✦ List priorities or commitments about which you have not clearly defined or communicated your loyalty.

Consider how you could use truth, abundance, and focused intent to bring yourself out of unhappiness and into love for yourself. I'm tempted to give examples here to guide you, but my intuition is telling me to refrain. This Personal Rulebook Play is designed to get you into the wisdom that resides in *your* Holy Grail. You have the answers within you, so take some quiet time to reflect, contemplate, and listen.

A few pieces of advice: Don't get too balled up trying to figure it out. Consciously play a game of Hide & Seek and have fun with it. If you start getting too serious or lost in your unhappy emotions, holler "Olly, Olly Oxen Free!" Use your defocus technique, and start the game back up when you're ready.

Treat it like a game. Life doesn't have to be hard; it can be your playground. Sorrow and similar emotions come from a scarcity perspective. This feeling of lack can make life seem hard, but those feelings close you off from your center and throw you off balance. It's your perspective that creates your experience. Use the only thing you can control—your perspective—to make it less complicated, demanding, and painful.

LIGHTEN UP . . . THEN LIGHT IT UP!

You practiced it in the above Personal Rulebook Play, and one lesson I hope you will gain from Retreat for Sanity is to lighten up. Life is supposed to be fun! That is the reason I chose to share these principles with you through the analogy of playing a game. When you were a child, you naturally wanted to have fun. It was easy to find ways to enjoy yourself. You didn't need things or money or even people to create fun in your world. It was the untarnished connection with *You* that made it possible. And throughout your life, you have closed off some, or most, of that connection and now it feels like *You* is hiding. The truth is that *You* has been there all along and is constantly and unwaveringly waiting for you to say, "Come out, come out, wherever you are!"

It is easiest for children to stay connected because they don't create tension, overanalyze, or care what others think about them. They just want to have fun and play and laugh and dance with life as it interacts with them. They also know when to have a time-out. Not the "time-outs" we enforce upon them as parents, but a true recess in order to refresh.

When my son Brayden, who was three years old at the time, went through a life-threatening illness, I witnessed the intuitive impulses that we humans are capable of having when we are in touch with ourselves. During his recovery he was very weak. He had lost ten pounds, which was a lot for a little guy who was only thirty-eight pounds at the beginning of the ordeal. He had lost so much muscle that he couldn't even walk without his little hips wobbling underneath him. His body had to build up stamina to get him back to the athletic, lively, exuberant bundle of energy he had been only three weeks prior.

We watched him desperately want to play and have fun. At first he could walk around for a minute or two, and then he would lie down on the floor (in the middle of the room) and take a break. He usually still wanted to interact in some way and play because his natural vitality was building within him. His body just had to catch up. Over the days and weeks to come, he slowly became stronger, but I will always remember observing the beauty of his ability to listen to his innate nature guiding him back to wholeness.

He didn't do it through fretting over why he wasn't getting better faster. He didn't do it by researching all of the things that would help him have stronger muscles and more energy. He did it by listening to the wisdom within him that guided him every step of the way— moment to moment, day after day, month after month, until he eventually returned to the dynamic, passionate, spicy little boy that he had always been.

My husband and I often smile now when he's pushing our buttons or running circles around us with his unlimited energy and joy. Before he was sick, I remember thinking, *I wish he would be a little less busy.* Now I have such appreciation for his vitality and energy. The thought that crosses my mind instead is, *What a beautiful gift he is to the world, even when he is driving me crazy!*

My son was able to connect with the *You* within him and not worry about how his healing process would unfold. Likewise, we can be easier with our approach to our own healing, relationships, or our dreams for achievement. I read an article somewhere that called America the "No Vacation Nation." It talked about how Americans don't take time to recharge. My husband and I have enjoyed traveling all over the world. Through meeting people from various countries, we have found this clearly to be the perception others have of Americans. And I believe it to be a justified one.

When we travel, we often take a minimum two-week vacation. The first time we did it we went to New Zealand. I remember thinking, *This is going to be such a long vacation!* When we would tell fellow Americans we were going to be gone for two weeks, they were so impressed (and a little baffled, I think) that we could leave for such a long time. But when we were in New Zealand and had conversations with those we met, their response to our length of vacation was almost one of disappointment for us that we *only* had two weeks. Most of the people we met were on holiday, as they say, for at least three weeks. Most of the time it was four to six weeks.

This first exposure revealed to me that I'd been "trained" to believe that taking time for recharging and just enjoying life was not a priority in my country. But discovery is the name of any Hide & Seek game, right? It became the opening for me to find out what I wanted. It was the stimulus that made me wonder how it would make me feel if I took more time to relax, regain clarity, and recharge. It was a situation that created the opportunity for me to practice the concept of stillness and activity, to find balance, to ask "Why not?" and apply my knowledge of savoring my journey, to gain more clarity by shifting my mental outlook toward abundance and opportunity as I engaged in my life with integrity. It was a multitude of Hide & Seek games in one! And it helped me become a master of my own life.

Every situation in your life can be a MASTERY game to help you become one with the whole of who you are. When you have more fun with the games and choose to lighten up, your games will give you opportunities to light up your world.

Personal Rulebook Play
MY APPROACH TO LIFE

Get out your Personal Rulebook, and use this Play to see if you can recognize your current approach to life. Do you take a lighthearted approach? Or are you very serious and heavyhearted about life's situations? To find out, respond to the following questions and do the visualization activities:

✦ What situation in your life right now is causing you some degree of stress?

✦ What are three reasons you feel stressed about the situation?

✦ What are three things you could say to yourself to take a more light-hearted approach to the situation?

✦ Turn the situation into a cartoon in your mind and play it through three times, making it as animated and fun as possible. Add fun music, play out a crazy sequence of events (like the old coyote and road runner cartoons), and imagine it in vibrant color.

✦ Now, take the situation, slow it down, make it black and white, and make it very serious. Imagine the image—like a TV screen in your mind—getting smaller and smaller as it moves farther and farther away from you until it disappears out of your sight or you no longer feel a strong connection to it.

✦ Notice how you feel about the situation after going through these processes. Does it feel less stressful to you? Do you feel more lighthearted about it?

Use these processes to help you lighten up about life. There was a book years ago that really resonated with the masses called *Don't Sweat the Small Stuff*. The reason so many people loved this book is because it reminded them about something they already innately knew—life is supposed to be fun. So lighten up . . . then go out into the world and light it up!

RETREAT INTO YOU

When you retreat, you find sanity because it is when you go inward that you find yourself, your Spirit, the *You,* in your MASTERY games of Hide & Seek. It is the iceberg we talked about in the conclusion to Chapter 5: Achieve through Alignment. The tip of the iceberg is the physical you and the larger nonphysical *You* is below the surface. When the ocean is filled with turbulent waves, the tip of the iceberg is among the chaos. But when you retreat beneath the surface where the greater part of *You* resides, you find calm, you find peace, you find serenity . . . you find sanity.

As you've learned in this part of the book, you need the fluctuation of engaging and retreating. We all thrive when we are challenged to become a more expanded person. We also thrive when we take time to release resistance, relax, regain clarity, and then go back to our activity.

You must now find the balance you need between the two in order for you to thrive. Have fun with it. If you feel like you've "lost" one game because you are out of balance, call out, "Olly Olly Oxen Free!" and regain your footing, find your center, and start the game again.

PART FOUR

READY OR NOT,
HERE I COME!

CHAPTER TEN

You *A*RE THE *K*EY

*T*he fourth area of the MASTERY acronym consists of just one thing: One thing that we have been searching for throughout this entire *Hide & Seek* book. One thing that is the key to your dreams, the key to creating the life you want, and the key to finding true happiness and personal fulfillment. You guessed it . . . it's *You!* The fourth area of the MASTERY game is you saying, "Ready or not, here I come!" to the world.

Just like when you are playing the childhood game of Hide & Seek, you don't know what you are about to experience. You don't have to have all the answers before you start. The purpose of playing the game is to experience what unfolds. You are simply counting and beginning to seek. Any game can bring suspense, excitement, exhilaration, and disappointment to those involved. Your MASTERY games of Hide & Seek are no different. They will bring you tears of joy and tears of sorrow. They will turn your stomach upside down and cause your heart to race. They will transport you to a place of exhilaration or ecstasy. And at some point, they will leave you feeling disappointed or discouraged. Yet through each game, you have the privilege and honor of finding yourself. You are able to dive into the depths of your soul, to discover the meaning of your life, and to feel the worthiness that is yours when you choose to accept and love everything about you.

Who is "you"? Well, just as we have been discovering throughout all the MASTERY games, there are two "yous." There is the you that is your physical personality, your body, your brain, your ego, etc. And then there is *You*: the spiritual you, your inner being, your center, or your true Self. These two "yous" make up the iceberg that is the whole of who you are. Without feeling the connection between your physical self and your spiritual self, you will not find absolute contentment, fulfillment, or worthiness. I'm hoping those words will help you feel the enormity of what I'm going for here. Your connection with the foundation of all that you are is bigger than anything else you will ever discover on this earth. What's even more exciting is that when you find that connection, EVERYTHING that you discover here on earth will be enhanced because of the solid core from which you live.

You can become a master in different areas of your life, but this game of hide and seek is the Ultimate Game of Personal MASTERY. It is about the broader picture. It is about learning how to accept yourself *and* express yourself to the fullest extent, so that you can bring all of yourself to the world. This is MASTERY with a Y, because without *You,* the word *mastery* doesn't exist. It is incomplete. Many people are going through life feeling incomplete with a desire to "find themselves." They are searching for the meaning—or purpose—of their lives. They want to feel the personal satisfaction that comes from feeling worthy of success or abundance or love. What they don't always understand is that all of those "goals" are achieved if, or when, they find the *You* within them. Personal mastery comes when *You* is added into all of your life's experiences. And the awe within your experience comes from an undeniable knowing of the sublime grandness that is *You*.

Your Hide & Seek games are simply your life experiences. They are countless opportunities for you to explore, to get lost, and to play. They are the ultimate games of personal mastery because they're filled with literally anything you can imagine. You choose how you experience your life. You choose your perspective. You choose your playground. You choose who you play with. All of these elements are what make your games uniquely yours.

Your Hide & Seek games
are simply your life experiences.

The reason I have encouraged you to look at your life as a series of games is because every experience you have is an opportunity for you to find yourself and bring all that you are into the world. You bring a unique set of gifts, talents, and perspectives that no one else in the entire world can bring. That means you are *numero uno*, at the top of the list, of over 7.15 *billion* people! No one else has experienced the life you've lived. No one else has come from your exact background or been through your hardships and achievements. No one else's mind processes situations or facts the same way yours does. Everything about you is uniquely yours, which is why your MASTERY games of Hide & Seek are also unique. Just during the course of reading this book, you have played many games and created your own Personal Rulebook Plays that are uniquely yours. All of these have been opportunities to find yourself and discover all that you have to give to the world.

I hope that you feel proud of the insights you've gained during these MASTERY games. I hope you have discovered that there is a wealth of worthiness within you, waiting for you to tap into it, and from which you can feel total satisfaction.

GO PLAY THE GAME

So now it is time for you to get out there and play. You know the rules. You're "IT," and you are looking for *You* within every part of your life. By practicing the ideas and processes from your Personal Rulebook Plays, you have begun to discover how to skillfully balance the Y characteristics and achieve true fulfillment in life—at work, at home, in relationships, and within yourself.

- ~ Maximize Your Impact

- ~ Achieve through Alignment

- ~ Savor the Journey

- ~ Think with Compassion

- ~ Engage with Integrity

- ~ Retreat for Sanity

- ~ *You* Are the Key

You have started becoming a skilled practitioner of the art of *You*. You now have a better understanding about what brings you happiness, a sense of purpose, success, health, contentment, awareness, self-respect, self-worth, and confidence.

The MASTERY game of Hide & Seek is made up of four areas:

- ~ Learning the Game

- ~ Discovering Your Truth

- ~ Finding the Balance

- ~ You Are the Key

You now have an understanding of what each of these areas means to your life (aka your game). The insights that have unfolded for you as you have taken the time to learn the game and have been willing to open yourself up to discover your personal truths will continue to bring you deeper personal satisfaction and acceptance of yourself. The appreciation that you now have for the need to find balance in your life, and knowing what that balance looks like for you, is going to give you the ability to have more compassion for yourself and others. Finally, your awareness that *You* are the key to everything is going to bring you to a level of personal mastery that the majority of people in the world dream about finding but are never able to grasp.

IT'S NOT ABOUT DISCIPLINE . . .
IT'S ABOUT CONSISTENCY!

Begin by doing exactly what you have been doing as you have been reading *Hide & Seek*. Create awareness around the situations and circumstances in your life. Treat your life's experiences as games that you are playing to find your flow. See everything as a chance to practice incorporating the whole of who you are. Give yourself the flexibility to stop any game and regain your footing when you need to. There are no limits to Olly Olly Oxen Free in your MASTERY games, so use them as often as you need them. That could be as simple as taking a few moments for yourself to breathe deeply and find your center.

Life is designed to be dynamic. If it wasn't dynamic, it would be boring, and boring games stink! They are not fun to play and they are not fun to watch. Look at your life as a dynamic and fun game that is giving you a chance to practice being consistent. Not consistent in the sense that every day is similar or that every game plays out the same way, but consistent in the sense that you are regularly looking for the same feeling of self-satisfaction throughout each day.

You can be disciplined in your life and work really hard to make things happen or to achieve certain goals, but discipline can often lead to self-judgment and feelings of disappointment or regret. These are not the outcomes that will lead you to personal mastery. Personal mastery comes through consistency. It is when you are able to be flexible like water, to be forceful like fire, and to be forgiving like a gentle breeze that you will become the master of your life. Mastery is not about discipline . . . it's about consistency!

> *Personal mastery comes through consistency.*
> *It is when you are able to be flexible like water,*
> *to be forceful like fire, and to be forgiving like a gentle*
> *breeze that you will become the master of your life.*

LOVE YOUR LIFE!

When I introduced myself at the beginning of this book, I shared with you that there was a time when I didn't have the ability to connect with the real me. The missing piece to my life puzzle was that ability to connect with an authenticity that came from the most primary part of my true Self.

I was living my life reactively, trying to access the feeling of happiness through success, people, or other things. From the outside, my life looked like the picture-perfect scenario, and truthfully, it was! The problem is that I wasn't in a place—mentally, emotionally, or spiritually—where I could appreciate it. When I was sitting in the sunshine, on the deck of my beautiful home saying to a friend, "I have such an amazing life, but I'm just not happy," *that* was a game-changing moment. I called out "Olly Olly Oxen Free!" and didn't even know I was playing a hide and seek game!

It was a realization that something big was missing from my life. I had all the external stuff that is admired by people in the world and touted to bring happiness. Those things are wonderful to have in your life, but without knowing the *You* that is at the core of your being, you will still feel empty inside. As amazing as all those things can be, they are meaningless if you don't feel the unconditional love that comes from the *You* within.

You will love your life when you start living it authentically. You will find that as you connect to your true Self, your perspective toward everything and everyone in your life will stem from appreciation. That appreciation will lead to more people, places, and things in your life for which you can feel grateful. People will think that you are happy because you have such a fantastic life. What they will fail to understand is that you have a fantastic life *because* you are happy. The happiness starts from the inside out. Start loving your life for absolutely all that it is—the good, the bad, and the ugly. When you do, you will discover the awe, you will align with the *You* in your Hide & Seek games, and together . . . you and *You* will embark on the supreme odyssey as your life becomes your playground.

Here's to you . . . and *You!*

ACKNOWLEDGMENTS

This book grew out of my journey of personal growth and self-discovery. Along the way, many people have supported and encouraged me, and I am indebted to them. To the following, I am especially grateful:

To my husband, Chris Bruntz, thank you for always encouraging me along my journey/cheering me on in my hide and seek game to find ME, and for being a daily example of making your life your playground.

To my sons, Taylor and Brayden, you each have taught me how to play my own Hide & Seek games in ways that only kids can do. Thank you for being the beautiful bright lights that you are. I love you both!

To my family, Mom, Dad, Tara, and Chad, there are no words to express my love and gratitude for everything you have been to me and my journey.

To Lisa McCourt, thank you for your editing guidance and magical touch.

To Kim Johnson, thank you for your "mad skills" and ability to help me find clarity. This book became a reality because of your desire and commitment to help me sift through the ideas in my mind. I will forever appreciate your guidance and coaching.

To Janis Miller and Laurie Rodgers, your love and unwavering belief in me is the true manifestation of friendship. I love you.

To Lynda Cherry and Jennifer Talbot, I am deeply grateful for your support and belief in this project. Thank you for your friendship and for scheduling my time and giving me the space to write so I could follow my dream.

To Carol Rosenberg and Gary Rosenberg, thank you for making the manuscript a beautiful masterpiece. Your abilities and passion for the work you do is unparalleled. Carol, your attention to detail and ability to pull it all together is extraordinary.

To Tristan Von Elrik, your commitment and artistic eye is truly amazing. Our journey of creative design has been a blast! And along the way, a lovely friendship emerged.

To Leo Lam, you are a photographic genius. Thank you for capturing my Essence so that I can now inspire others to embrace theirs.

To Chris Widener, thank you for challenging me and offering critical feedback whether it was convenient or not! Ha Ha! Your expertise and friendship have been a wonderful part of this endeavor.

To my clients, mentors, teachers, and coaches who have taught me more through our relationships than any intellectual book could ever attempt, thank you.

And finally, to those of you I hope now feel inspired and prepared to create personal MASTERY in your life, my very best wishes. You have chosen a worthy path. May you find . . . YOU!

Kami

ABOUT THE AUTHOR

Karri Bruntz is a best-selling author, speaker, financial advisor, and coach dedicated to living life authentically and inspiring others to do the same. For nearly two decades, she has been coaching high-net-worth clients through the ups and downs of the stock market. This has been no easy feat, but without these experiences, Karri would not have been able to discover her inner strengths and embrace her true Self.

Karri's personal life experiences sparked her desire for success through personal growth, which led to her discovery of universal truths and her powerful belief in a holistic approach to work and play. She soon realized these truths were the secret to unlocking one's innate strengths, and once aligned properly, they would pave the path to a life full of vitality, confidence and extraordinary prosperity.

Living life as a student and continuously putting the tools she learns to work in her own life have resulted in Karri's recognized success among all financial advisors. That success has allowed her to fulfill another passion to help women embrace their whole self and stand with confidence in all areas of their life.

Due to her holistic approach in business, Karri has been invited to speak at many events to thousands of men and women in the workplace. Her topics have included Wholeness in the Workplace; Three A's of Success: Authenticity, Awareness, Action; Discover Your Strengths and Ignite Your Power; Unleash Your Mojo; and Hide and Seek: How Do You Win the Game?

Karri has hosted her own radio show in Seattle and organized large events centered on health, well-being, and personal growth. She continues to train and inspire teams in the corporate world and personally coaches women who want to learn how to use their natural talents to create confidence and success in their personal life and career. To empower more women to discover their unique talents and find their confidence to take on their greatest ambitions, Karri and her team are continually creating products and free resources on her website: www.KarriBruntz.com.

Karri lives in the Seattle area with her husband, Chris, and two children, Taylor and Brayden.

Made in the USA
Columbia, SC
19 September 2019